Form and Purpose

To Ruth Whyte
with best wishes

Moshe Safdie

Aspen June 21/84

Books by Moshe Safdie

For Everyone a Garden
Beyond Habitat
Form and Purpose

Form and Purpose

MOSHE SAFDIE

Edited by John Kettle

Houghton Mifflin Company Boston   1982

Library of Congress Cataloging in Publication Data

Safdie, Moshe, date
    Form and purpose.
    Bibliography: p.
    1. Architectural design.   2. Functionalism (Archi-
tecture)   I. Kettle, John.   II. Title.

NA2750.S22   1981   729   81-6789
ISBN 0-395-31663-4   AACR2
ISBN 0-395-31664-2 (pbk.)

Printed in the United States of America

V 10 9 8 7 6 5 4 3 2 1

Research and publication sponsored by the Design Arts Program, National
Endowment for the Arts, through a grant to the International Design Education Foundation.

Book design by David Ford

Acknowledgments

In 1969, John Kettle and I collaborated for the purpose of chronicling the story of the building of Habitat. John, who had been editor of *The Canadian Architect,* edited our conversations into what became *Beyond Habitat.* Ten years later, in the fall of 1979, we met again, this time to talk about *Form and Purpose.* Once more John edited our conversations, and they form the core of this book. My thanks go to him for the patience and energy he has devoted to this task.

My thanks also go to Judy Bing, who researched and collected the illustrations; to Dorothy O'Carroll, my assistant for the 1980 Aspen Design Conference, who assisted in the research and preparation of the manuscript; and to William Gillitt, my associate of many years, for reviewing the manuscript and suggesting many clarifications.

In addition, my appreciation is to be expressed to Dick Farson, outgoing president of the International Design Conference in Aspen (IDCA), and to Jane Thompson and Ralph Caplan, members of the Board of IDCA and its Publications Committee, for reviewing some

of the chapters and making suggestions, and, above all, for their
encouragement.

Finally, I want to indicate my gratitude to the Design Arts Program, National Endowment for the Arts, for making this book possible — first, for awarding me a Project Fellowship Grant in 1979, which enabled me to carry out the initial writing and research for the book, and second, for a Cooperative Agreement given to the International Design Education Foundation, which made possible the initial printing of this book as part of the 1980 Aspen design conference.

Contents

Acknowledgments   v

Introduction   ix

1/Design in Nature   1

2/The Indigenous Builders   21

3/The Sophisticated Builders   49

4/Art, Fashion, and Style   67

5/City Fabric   101

6/Contemporary Diagnosis   117

Notes   139

Selected Bibliography   141

Credits   143

Introduction

Every day each of us makes design decisions. We select a shirt and tie, or blouse and skirt, out of the closet; we go to the store to buy clothing; we buy and arrange furniture; select a car; purchase or rent a house or apartment. Sometimes we can exercise considerable choice, sometimes we face frustrating limitations, but, nevertheless, design decisions we make.

Those of us in the design professions not only make such decisions for ourselves but, of course, make them for others. We propose designs for people's clothing, household goods, furniture, buildings, even cities.

For both the lay person and the design professional, these daily decisions seem to follow an increasingly erratic, irrational, or at least unpredictable path. Sometimes we act out of insecurity, considering other people's opinions of our decisions; sometimes out of an urge for originality or novelty; sometimes to proclaim our status; and sometimes, if not quite often enough, out of consideration of performance, comfort, well-being, and what genuinely gives us pleasure.

This book will attempt to deal with these questions at their most fundamental level — the connection between design, motivation, and values. The book has been written, in part, as a response to the present debate over the course architecture should take, but it attempts to transcend the immediate discussion, so that in the end each of us (myself included) will create with clearer purpose.

The seed for this book was planted in Montreal in the spring of 1978. The Board of Directors of the International Design Conference in Aspen was meeting there and, as an adviser to the Board, I was invited to participate. George Nelson and I were sitting on the roof terrace of the Hotel Bonaventure, chatting, when he first approached me about taking on the chairmanship of the Aspen Design Conference for 1980. I had just accepted Harvard's invitation to become director of the urban-design program at the Graduate School of Design and was in the process of moving my office to Boston. Engaged in two full-time jobs, I was being offered a third.

Yet the same reason that had led me to accept Harvard's invitation also persuaded me, perhaps against my better judgment, to accept George's challenge. The architectural profession was drifting. New attitudes, manifestoes, and design proposals were being published. The journals were filled with works that seemed to me to express a general withdrawal — indeed, a reversal — from a longtime commitment to values that expressed a concern for people and their needs; values that supported the creation of the best living environment possible in the face of a multitude of constraints — economic, technical, and political; values that aimed at improving the manmade environment. Instead I felt that a growing number of architects had found solace in dealing with architecture as an abstract undertaking, a personal and private art. The commitment to social and community issues that was dominant in the sixties seemed to have made an about-face. Daniel Bell put his finger on this when he wrote that

the cultural realm is one of self-expression and self-gratification. It is anti-institutional and antinomian in that the individual is taken to be the measure of satisfaction, and his feelings, sentiments, and judgments, not some objective standard of quality and value, determine the worth of cultural objects. At its most blatant, this sentiment asks of a poem, a play, or a painting, not whether it is good or meretricious, but "What does it do for me?"[1]

It was shortly after this that the publication of Philip Johnson's American Telephone and Telegraph building first appeared in the media. Johnson's building, and, even more important, his explanation of it, appeared to be an attempt at legitimizing the new attitudes in the profession. I could not resist commenting, and in a moment of passion I wrote to him:

May 16, 1978

Dear Philip:

I wrote to you about two years ago after visiting the IDS Center in Minneapolis, to congratulate you on what I thought was a wonderful achievement, a place which responds to an unsatisfied need to relate people to low and tall buildings in the city. Now I must write to you to voice my concern over your recently published design for the AT&T Building in New York. I do so in friendship and respect for much of what you have done in the past, and in disagreement over the position you now seem to be taking.

It is, of course, dangerous to judge a building from a newspaper photograph, but from all that has been quoted and said about it, I feel I can at least comment on your declared intentions. So many important issues exist from the base to the roof of a tall building which I would like to challenge. This attitude which is emerging within the profession, and which you here seem to be endorsing, has pushed me towards returning to teaching.

If I were to attempt to summarize what I consider this attitude to be, I would say it is a preoccupation with the arbitrary, purely visual aspects of a building as the main generative consideration in its formation. This formalistic (and sometimes eclectic) visual game, in which there are no rules, is motivated sometimes by whim, humor or desire to shock, and sometimes by boredom or nostalgia. It appears not to be based on any consideration of lifestyle, let alone on the materials, processes, and physical realities which underline the *raison d'être* of building.

Your recent "act" for the AT&T Building would probably not usually evoke all this discussion, being one of many buildings you have designed, except that it appears as an endorsement of an attitude with which I have passionately come to disagree. As for this trend, I should say that even if one accepts the premise of many of those who have come to be called Postmodern architects, it seems to me that, at a purely intuitive level, much of it is not very exciting form-making, even if one was prepared to disassociate it from my great concern for the fundamental question of responsibility.

I cannot agree more with the statements attributed to you that the so-called international style, and much built in the name of modern architecture, has lacked richness. It seems that it was in the fundamental oversimplification by which these buildings denied so many basic aspects of their morphology that we have come to understand them as lacking. It was the poor "fitness to purpose," purpose being the very broad array of physical and psychic needs, which brought about our dissatisfaction with contemporary buildings. It is ironical that historical buildings, spurned in the '30s and the '40s, are now recognized to possess a more integrated response to environmental needs. I realize that I am using a lot of shorthand terms to express myself which require explanation, but I hope that you know what I am trying to say.

It is in an understanding of the shortcomings of the architecture of the last thirty or forty years that, I believe, lie the seeds for growth and positive evolution of architecture. It is by broadening the base of the considerations of the form-making process, not by ignoring them or substituting whim and whimsy, that we shall move forward.

I really believe that there are so many important issues requiring understanding and resolution that should form the basis for our collective efforts. To start with, we have yet to understand the process by which what we build in the urban environment relates to the rest of the city so as to fulfill the principle of "the sum being greater than the individual parts." In the past, it has been demonstrated that the quality of the environment in the city derived from the fact that groups of buildings formed better environments, such as the city square, the bazaar or the street. Buildings possessed common denominators, but our understanding of these common denominators and our ability to relate what we are doing to the rest of the city today leaves so much to be desired. Such common denominators can only emerge from what I would term, in the absence of a better expression, things which are "organically truthful" in their response to individual and collective needs. This is beginning to sound like a treatise, which it is not meant to be, but I feel I have to identify concerns which need to be dealt with.

The same is true for processes and materials. We are obviously at the beginning of new developments. The visual and formal expression of new processes is bound, as it has been in the past, to create great riches. As for materials, it appears to me that here, too, we are on the verge of a breakthrough. We seem to be getting closer to the point where new materials can make increasingly possible the realization of a contemporary Garden of Eden.

These issues have always existed, but there are those which are very special to our own era. There are the problems of dealing with great numbers, and the problems of dealing with the effect of bureaucracy. To put it positively, how do we deal with the issues of identity, of scale, of comfort, of the relationship to nature, notwithstanding the great masses for whom we are building, and the enormous density, size, and scale, both vertical and horizontal, of our cities? These questions demand inventiveness, slow, painstaking evolutionary improvement, patience and, most important, a motivation based on the concern for the well-being of those for whom we build. This does not leave much room for maneuvering arbitrarily. This does not leave much freedom of action.

In Paul Goldberger's article on you in the Sunday *New York Times,* he wrote at the end: "Whether the public is really ready for this style is another question." Coming from the *New York Times* architectural critic, who really should know better, a reference to style similar to that expected from a *Vogue* fashion writer on the latest proposals of a Parisian fashion house was a surprise. How often, it seems, have we been confronted with such questions by our clients, and how difficult it has been to deal with them.

Also, when reading the *Times* article, I realized that our dialogue on

the subject has been continuing for quite some time. Goldberger quotes
you: "There is only one absolute today and that is change . . ." It
sounded familiar, and I remembered that I had quoted this very sentence
somewhere in my writings. I looked for it and found it in *Beyond Habitat,*
on page 169:

"So, I basically disagree with Philip Johnson, who says everything is
possible in architecture today: 'There are no rules, surely no certainties in
any of the arts. There is only the feeling of a wonderful freedom.'

"I absolutely disagree with him. We have very few alternatives to the
right solution. Only by being totally arbitrary is it possible to have no
rules and complete freedom. In terms of the forces and realities of life
today, a solution is a process of moving towards a truth, which is the complete opposite of freedom from rules."

I have been rather long-winded in trying to say that if our energies
were wholly directed to making a city, a building, a place, the rediscovery
of the Garden of Eden, we would not need to indulge in frivolities. You,
who have spent so many years searching for this Garden, seem to be at
this point sending others on a goosechase. Yours, with much friendship
and warm wishes,

Moshe Safdie

A few days later I received his response:

June 7, 1978

Dear Moshe:

I had no idea that we differed so much in our basic philosophy of
architecture. *Eclecticism* is not a bad word to me. *Visual aspects* of a building seem, to me, primary (are my arches more "arbitrary" than your
arches in Jerusalem?). In counterdistinction to the theoreticians of the
heroic period, it seems to me that form is everything. The very *raison
d'être* of a building seems to me to be *form.* As far as fitness of purpose
is concerned, the AT&T building is eminently functional. Every floor was
designed with the 5-foot modules so beloved by interior planners. The
100 by 200 foot space is just what a speculative builder would build if
he could.

To me, we are evolving in modern architecture, and the AT&T building is an example of this evolution. I would not build the same building in Houston, of course, but the new interest in the context of the city, in the history of the city, and thirdly, the symbolic meaning of telephone in the city all demand form like AT&T with its neo-Renaissance detail, its derivations from the twenties, and its functional raising of the building from the street.

You are kind to take so much time to write me your thoughts. I hope when you are in New York you will continue to dialogue. I hope I can visit Jerusalem again to see your great work there.

Very respectfully yours,
Philip Johnson

And the debate goes on.

Form and Purpose became the theme for a conference and the title for a book. But, as happens with titles, it assumed a life of its own. The conference, as I first conceived of it, was to be primarily a platform for debating the issues facing architecture. But one could not deal with form and purpose without investigating the relationship of form to purpose in nature; without reviewing the history of their relationship in manmade design throughout the centuries; without exploring the basic human urges to decorate, and to celebrate the phenomenon of ritual; and, last but not least, without confronting the omnipresent force of fashionability, the striving for novelty and constant change. So if, on the one hand, there were the words of D'Arcy Thompson who had inspired me in my youth, there was also the other side. As Catherine Bateson put it in *Our Own Metaphor:*

Attempts have been made in the last hundred years to create social systems with a minimum of symbolic, supernatural, and ritual components. Education has been secularized, and so on. But could a social system be viable with only laws and ethical principles and no fantasy, no play, no art, no totemism, no religion, and no humor?[2]

Whenever I got confused in writing this book, whenever I felt that I did not have the perspective needed to distinguish the trees from the forest, I imagined myself to be a Martian arriving in a spaceship to spy on Earth — an idea I had gathered from a wonderful animated film made by the National Film Board of Canada. In the film the Martians arrive by air. Their attention is focused on what they perceive to be the dominant species of the planet Earth — a creature made of metal, mounted on wheels, that traverses urban settlements and the countryside with some speed. The Martian report gives considerable detail on the behavior of these creatures, and at the end presents an unresolved issue. It is observed that there are two-legged parasites that inhabit these wheeled creatures. "We have not been able to determine yet," the report states, "what purpose these parasites serve."

At certain moments I put myself in that ship. Cities, patterns of settlement, and streets suddenly take on another character. This attitude resembles what one might have in examining the innards of an anthill or a coral formation. In moments of detachment, one can pose all kinds of sacrilegious questions — questions about the values we put on things. One hundred thousand dollars for paint spread on canvas. Our compulsive urge to discard and make new, discard and make new. Our rather recent mania for never doing anything the same way twice. Our commitment to change, our embarrassment at repetition — all coming at a time when by any measure whatsoever there is meteoric change in science and technology and each decade is equivalent to a century or even a millennium in the past. Yet when it comes to design — the design of our environment, cities, buildings, houses, utensils, clothes, furniture, cars, and planes — there is one overriding test: Is it done with a deep sense of commitment to people, a commitment in the broadest sense to man in all his complexities — his desires, hopes, fears, and, above all, his well-being? It is a surprisingly simple test.

Moshe Safdie

1 Design in Nature

Plants respond to climate and the cycles of the seasons. They shed their leaves to withstand the cold and grow a new set when the sun and warmth return.

QUITE EARLY in my architectural education, I was introduced to the works of D'Arcy Thompson, who, at the end of the nineteenth century, originated the study of morphology. In his two-volume work *Growth and Form,* Thompson shows how the forms and structures of nature, with all their complexity, richness, intricacy, and beauty, evolved in response to an organism's will to survive.[3]

Andreas Feininger, in his book *Anatomy of Nature,*[4] illustrates this responsiveness in the elaborate structures of plants, animals, and geological formations, demonstrating an inspired understanding of their reason for being. I always feel embarrassed when comparing these examples to our primitive and inadequate response to equally complex needs and requirements in the manmade environment.

Consider the way many plants respond to climate and the cycles of the seasons. They shed their leaves to withstand the cold, and grow a new set when the sun and warmth return. They meet severe requirements with convertibility. Then look at our manmade environment: It is static; the notion that public spaces might be enclosed with glass to capture the sunlight and protect people in winter, and might be open to the air in summer, is considered a fantasy. Instead we withdraw into a controlled interior environment of air-conditioned bliss.

Every form in nature has, built into it, the ability to grow and to change. As the nautilus grows, the hard shell of its "house" remains in constant proportion to its body, building on the nuclear structure without discarding what was there in the first place. D'Arcy Thompson illustrates most elegantly how this growth pattern results in a logarithmic spiral.

Not only does the nautilus expand proportionately in what is known as gnomonic growth, but it uses the previous chambers for buoyancy so that it may float at different levels in the sea. Often in nature one element has two or three functions: redundancy and duplication, integrative design.

But that is only one example of growth in nature. The principles of growth in the human body are quite different. For instance, there is

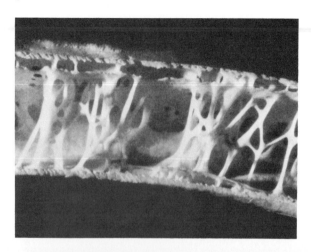

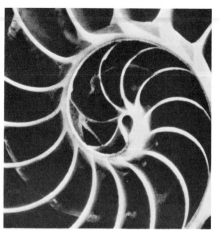

Left:
The bone structure of the wing of the vulture, which requires great strength with minimum weight, is a most beautiful three-dimensional lattice.

Right:
Every form in nature has, built into it, the ability to grow and to change. As the nautilus grows, the shell remains in constant proportion to its body, building on the nuclear structure. D'Arcy Thompson illustrates most elegantly how this growth pattern results in a logarithmic spiral.

Below:
The mulberry leaf as observed by Peter Stevens.

the constant need for repair. We cut our hand, and new cells repair the cut; we constantly have cells dying and new cells replacing them. Through widespread replacement of cells throughout the organism's body, we deal with growth quite differently than the nautilus.

With the expansion that cities experience, we continually have to deal with increases in size, growth of population and institutions, and growth of the parts within the whole. Sometimes the growth of the parts is out of proportion to the whole. There is also the need for constant repair and replacement. But in the city we have been unable to achieve a method of accommodating growth and change in a way that is as effective and elegant as that of the nautilus or the human body.

In nature, the more severe the problem, the more intricate and complex — and indeed beautiful — the solution. The bone structure of the wing of the vulture, for instance, which requires great strength with minimum weight, is a most beautiful three-dimensional lattice. Nature is diverse. It does not attempt to solve with rigidity what can be solved with elasticity. The wheat stalk and the tree are designed to "give," to bend to the point where the force of the wind is minimized, and then to resume their upright positions. The airplane similarly adopts this principle. Rigid airplanes simply couldn't take off, because of the weight, and so we design wings that in large planes move four or five feet at the tips, to absorb the forces elastically.

In contrast, however, we design rigid buildings. The notion that a thirty-story building should move when the wind hits it, and sway a little bit, seems shocking. Our designs in response to nature's forces are primitive in comparison to nature's own designs.

For these reasons I have always found it inspiring to study the constructions of indigenous builders and to examine the evolution of forms in nature, where I am perpetually confronted with the intimate connection between *form* and *purpose.*

This does not mean that we can or should adapt the forms of nature to buildings. One cannot arrange houses in a high-rise structure, like the leaves on an elm tree, or work out a structural system to

The wheat stalk and the tree are designed to "give," to bend to the point where the force of the wind is minimized, and then to resume their upright position. The airplane similarly adopts this principle. The *Gossamer Condor,* designed by Paul MacCready.

support a large span, in imitation of a vulture's wing — or for that matter design a city in the form of a logarithmic spiral. This would be arbitrary formalism — adopting shapes and structures because one has been seduced by their beauty, rather than attempting to evolve forms that are responsive to the needs, requirements, and specifications of the manmade object or environment. In studying forms in nature, we search for an understanding of the principles behind them; we must always seek the connection between the form and its purpose.

But every time I design a building, after attempting to define what is fundamental to the "survival of the organism" and exploring forms that evolve in response — in a sense attempting to imitate a process that has evolved over millennia in nature — I wonder if this is possible for us. Can we imitate Darwinian evolution? Can we recognize the great number of requirements, and can our minds synthesize them?

When looking at beautiful and intricate shells, plants, or the varieties of housing that animals build for themselves (nests, beehives, beaver dams, coral, or spider webs), we note their origin in physical principles. They are concerned with material, gravity, reproduction, and food and digestion; in other words, they are involved with the physical survival of the organism.

In regard to the requirements of an environment for man, however, while the same physical requirements and forces are undoubtedly present, it would appear that there are other dimensions as well, which cannot be defined in physical terms. A church is constructed for worship: It requires a sense of environment that supports and evokes this category of human experience, something that does not have precedent among the organisms of nature. The manmade environment here combines with physical forces, in response to psychic effects or needs, in a way that does not occur in nature and that adds a dimension of complexity. This is a recurring theme: Once we recognize that our environment is formed by both physical and

Man does not live by bread alone. Throughout history we have devoted a tremendous amount of energy, imagination, and creativity to making elaborate combinations of ingredients. Cuisine is based on satisfying one's palate and transcends the issue of physical survival. The cat kills the mouse and eats it; it doesn't stew it in mussel sauce and add cream and spices. *Below:* a gourmet platter from Julia Child's kitchen.

psychic needs, we can assess whether these are accommodated in a complementary, harmonious way or whether their resolution is conflicting (that is, satisfies only a psychic need, as in a symbolic gesture that contradicts gravity or energy efficiency).

We sometimes assume that designs in primitive indigenous environments respond to basic physical needs only, but indigenous buildings are rich in decoration and symbolism. In almost every case, though, it can be demonstrated that this is achieved through the embellishment of essential building elements. Thus, for example, a grille needed for shading and permitting ventilation becomes an elaborate arabesque. Masonry vaulted construction becomes a symphony of geometrically structured domes. The need to surface the building provides the opportunity for pattern and color. This complementarity of elaboration and decoration on one hand and functional elements on the other is often reversed in affluent, sophisticated cultures. Thus because of formal preconceptions about façade proportions, windows of illogical size are placed in a room, or, a more contemporary example, all-glass buildings are constructed in the middle of a desert.

A similar set of questions is raised in relation to what are in fact psychic needs. Is fashion (the striving for fashionability or novelty and change) a response to a fundamental need of the human psyche, or is it the result of manipulation by interest groups that play on the insecurity of their fellow men? Similarly, if the origins of art are in ancient rituals, even superstitions, what is their relevant impact on the manmade environment as they evolve today?

Man does not live by bread alone. In order to survive, we need so many calories — so much fat and protein and vitamins. The food (that is, form) can be fairly simple. We need to consume only certain minimum ingredients. And yet throughout history we have devoted a tremendous amount of energy, imagination, and creativity to making elaborate combinations of these ingredients; the full range of the cuisine of many cultures is based on personal satisfaction and transcends the issue of physical survival. The cat kills the mouse and

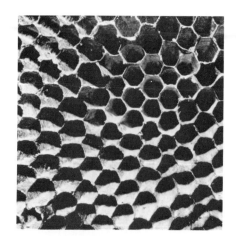

Above left:
A hornet's nest, by Andreas
Feininger. The hexagonal comb
provides maximum space and
strength with a minimum of
structure.

Compare the way buildings in
the city respond to sunlight with
the way plants do — for example, cacti that rotate continuously
to keep an edge to the sun, to
preserve their moisture (*above
right*) and olive leaves that turn
with the sun, facing their silver
sides to the light to reflect the
heat (*below*). In cooler climates, the spiral distribution
of branches and leaves allows
maximum exposure to the sun,
to enhance the process of
photosynthesis.

eats it: It doesn't stew it in mussel sauce and add cream and spices.
By doing all these things to our foods, we have transcended mere
survival.

When I was commissioned to design the Yeshiva Porat Joseph, the
rabbinical college in Jerusalem, one thing I realized was that I had
to deal with the problem of accommodating a new building to the
heart of historical Jerusalem. By "accommodating," I mean that out
of respect and deference to the site, the new building should appear
as though it had always been there. I didn't want anyone to be able
to say, "Ah, here was a group of people who wanted their building to
stand out from the rest of the city." The quality of accommodation
would not evolve out of any physical analysis of the problem or of
the climate or terrain; it had to do with a sense of continuity and of
culture. That is a dimension we don't find in D'Arcy Thompson.

Part of the Yeshiva was the synagogue. Up to that point I had designed houses, villages, and towns, and now for the first time I was
confronted with designing a place of worship. I don't usually go to
synagogue, although I recognize the possibility that sometime I may
want to. People go to synogogue wanting to be in a special place. I
also cherish the notion of Jews that any room can be a synagogue:
Put ten men together who want to worship, and the space becomes a
synagogue. But the idea of worshiping together in a special place
evokes something very important. Eventually I came to understand
that this had to do with a sense of place, with scale, and with light.
The interaction, even interpenetration, of space and light seems to
occur in almost all religious buildings. It calls to mind one of the first
passages in Genesis: "Let there be light."

Having said that design in nature has been inspiring, I must immediately add that I recognize the contribution the human psyche
makes: It creates dependence on symbol and the association of images
that is built into our memory. All of this comes from our forefathers
and is part of us. As Carl Sagan points out, our fear of snakes or of
heights — or, even more fundamentally, our feeling about a space —

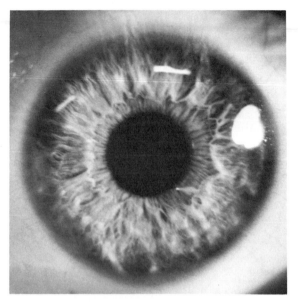

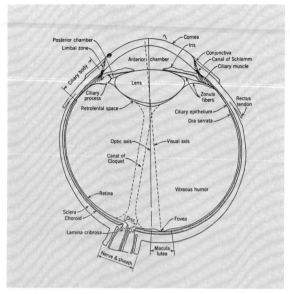

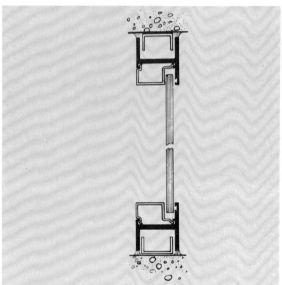

Our eye is a most sophisticated and efficient organism. It has a built-in cleaning system and is constantly being washed, and it can be shut off completely when we don't want to look out. Our pupil enlarges and contracts to accommodate the changing level of light.

cannot be understood without relating such feelings to mankind's experience of living in caves or trees, or to the evolution of the species.[5] We arrive here with a certain amount of emotional baggage, all of which becomes part of the requirements of design.

At the same time, I should emphasize that most manmade design doesn't come close to responding to the physical framework in the way natural organisms do. We have not even begun to evolve building forms and structures that have the kind of exactness, economy, or sophistication of response that natural organisms have. Simply compare the way buildings and spaces in the city respond to sunlight with the way plants do — for example, the sophistication of olive leaves that turn with the sun, facing their silver sides to the light to reflect the heat, and certain cacti that rotate continuously to keep an edge to the sun, to preserve their moisture. Or compare the spiral distribution of leaves in cooler climates, allowing maximum exposure to the sun, to enhance the process of photosynthesis. Compare any of these examples to the static character of our buildings that shadow public spaces, or to rooms that are pitilessly exposed to the sun in hot climates or face the sunless north in cold winter.

People seem simply to adapt to inconvenience. The office worker whose desk is located next to a glass wall on the south face of an all-glass building bakes in the sun. Consequently, we bully nature to make up for these grotesque distortions, using vast quantities of energy to cool places where the sun blazes through glass in summer; and six months later, when it is thirty degrees below zero outside, we use more energy to keep an acceptable temperature inside that glass wall.

Think of the eye. Our eye is a most sophisticated and efficient organism. It has an enclosure. It has a built-in cleaning system and is constantly being washed. It can be shut off completely when we don't want to look out. Our pupil enlarges and contracts to accommodate the changing level of light. Our eye is designed to turn in the direction we want to see; it can be focused near or far. We even have two eyes, so that we can measure distance.

The window should respond to conditions of night, day, sun, or clouds. It should enable us to look in different directions. It should enable shade-closing for privacy.

Now compare the eye to a window, which has many of the same requirements. For example, the window needs to deal with night, day, sun, or clouds. When we want to look out the window, we want to look in different directions. We also want to be able to shade the window, to shut it for privacy. There is the same need for focusing, the same need for almost all the demands we make on eyes. And what do we have? An opening with a transparent skin, in a masonry wall. Until recently we used shutters and louvers to control light, but now we don't even have shutters anymore. In many buildings we can't even open the windows for ventilation.

Somehow it seems that our ingenuity is better demonstrated in fields other than building. For instance, the telephone, with a few taps on the buttons, will carry a voice from a small town in Nebraska to a village in the Sahara. We can make a space vehicle that will go all the way to Mars, pick up rocks, photograph them, and send the pictures back in code. This kind of inventiveness and imagination is lacking in our building processes.

Design in nature offers us some very important lessons. First is a fundamental principle: If you seek responsiveness and fitness to purpose, you will achieve an order that we perceive as beauty; if you seek beauty for beauty's sake you will not achieve it, because you will not attain that order which in nature is considered fitness to purpose. A second principle is that we should forever look to nature as a measure of achievement in response to the physical demands of the environment. If we build a thirty-story structure, we should always ask ourselves, "In framing this structure, which has to withstand earthquakes and wind, have we used materials as economically as they are used in the vulture's wing?" As long as we can make the comparison, we have a measure that will inspire us to greater achievement.

In nature, economy is directly linked to survival. Nature does more with less, and the most with the least, subject to the *constraints of survival*. Because water is in short supply, nature finds a way for the cactus to conserve its moisture and to live on very little water, by cutting back to the absolute minimum the amount of moisture necessary for its survival.

Economy means finding the basic, minimum requirements. We have to understand what these minimum requirements are in the human environment; otherwise, we risk the danger of using the word *economy* erroneously. What are the basic, noncompromisable, mandatory requirements for the human environment? You might say, "One could make this house cheaper. It has a surface of a hundred square meters. If you make it fifty, it would be cheaper." The next question is, What constitutes an environment of well-being? What is survival? These questions are loaded with value judgments, because humanity is very adaptable. There are places where people would feel that unless they had a certain amount of space, say a room of two hundred square feet, they would be seriously deprived. At the same time, there are places where people are forced by necessity to live ten to a room of the same size and to accept it. Man is very adaptable, and, because of that, defining what is essential to well-being is difficult and the issue of economy becomes complex. Each society has to define this for itself and then strive to achieve it with minimum resources. There is no trick to doing the least with the least; anybody can do that. Anybody can take a house that is fifty square meters and build it for a cost that is less than a house of one hundred square meters. But there are ways of building a one-hundred-square-meter house that are economical and ways that are very uneconomical. Out of context, the giraffe's long neck appears to be uneconomical, but considering that its food supply grows high up on trees, the length of its neck is essential to the animal's survival.

Even if we could reach a level of sophistication that allowed us to respond to physical needs with nature's exactness, this response would not necessarily answer the spiritual and psychic needs of man. For example, we find that even in the most primitive environments, where basic shelter is obtained from mud bricks, leather, or the simplest materials (although these are sometimes used in sophisticated

Enlarged view of a Bell Labs-designed CDC fitter, showing chip features in detail. The telephone circuit. Nowhere is the contrast between the inflexible technology of the stamping machine and the open-ended technology of miniature circuitry more apparent than in our telephone system. Flexibility and choice are achieved through technology; with an effortless touch of the dial we can instantly reach any one of hundreds of millions of people anywhere in the world. Cannot technology do the same for the built environment?

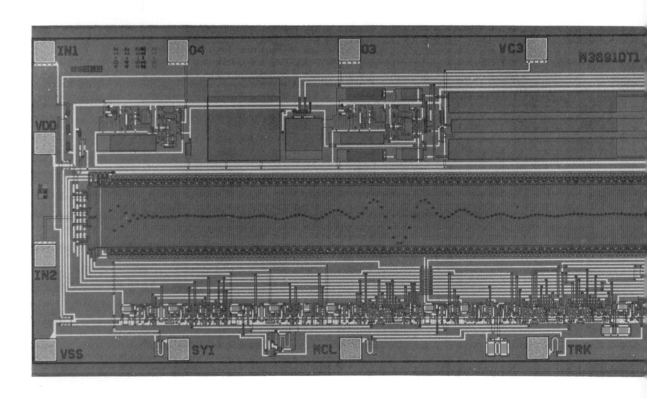

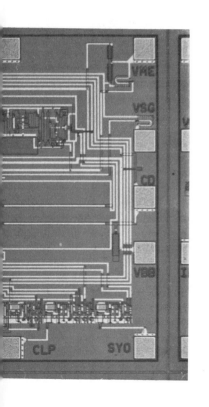

ways, as, for example, in the igloo), man does things that cannot be explained in terms of physical need. People extract seeds from plants and string them around their doors. They crush plants to make pigments to decorate their walls. They carve wooden doors and windows with intricate geometric decorative patterns. Here, sheer survival has been left behind and we have crossed a line to the other side, where there is a desire to decorate, to identify social hierarchies, to protect man from the evil eye, and to record and document. Similarly, as we have seen, in cooking an elaborate meal by adding spices and other ingredients to food, man enriches his experiences beyond the requirements for survival.

What is important to remember about these efforts in primitive societies is that they basically involved an individual's action for his own purposes. A person carves his own piece of wood to make an image to worship, and then makes a comb out of the leftover piece of wood. Art is not institutionalized to the point where the process of enrichment is delegated to others. Consequently, the whole issue of whether this enrichment is a meaningful process of design is answered automatically by the fact that the person who does it because it satisfies him also fulfills a higher purpose: that of enabling himself to take part in a ritual or ceremony.

When a man makes a shelter for himself, an immediate sense of economy is expressed in this architecture. He uses every mud brick to the limit of what it can do for him. But the power brokers don't live by the same rules. Darius, the King of Persia, who built Persepolis, and the pharaoh who built the great pyramid at Giza, were free of any notion of economy. Their acts of building had to do with the assertion of the status of the ruler, for which all kinds of energy and labor were mobilized. The architecture of palaces and temples has never been governed by the same forces of economy that affect a person building a shelter for himself. So the question arises, Is the building of a pyramid or a temple governed by the same laws that influence design in nature?

The pharaoh built a pyramid to protect his body and to guarantee

Left:
The architecture of palaces and
temples has never been governed
by the same forces of economy
that affect a person who builds a
shelter for himself. Is the building of a temple governed by the
same laws that influence design
in nature?

Right:
A house in Jaselmar, India: The
entire town — every house, public institution, palace, and temple — is built of carved stone that
looks almost like lace. Jaselmar
shows at once man's urge to
decorate, to impress, but at the
same time to develop a vernacular in which masonry walls
become screens, allowing the
cooling air to move through the
buildings.

himself life everlasting; the pyramid was a monument that could survive anything — an earthquake or any natural disaster. Whether this is interpreted as an act motivated by superstition and mysticism or viewed as a society's need to assert itself through symbols, it embodies a sense of survival. It is difficult to conceive that the tens of thousands of slaves who built the pyramids, and those who worked to provide them with food, would have submitted, unless they felt that in participating in the pharaoh's actions they too were somehow assuring "survival" for themselves. Similarly, in the construction of the great Gothic cathedrals any sense of economy was overshadowed by the collective will of a group of people to build a place of worship to God, who was the central object of their lives and their hope for survival.

There have always been individuals or groups in power whose architecture is concerned with the perpetuation of that power. It would be naive to ignore the fact that the institutional structure of older societies was a major determinant of the building expression of their times. We can see that in the past the majority of man's construction evolved with a close interrelationship between form and purpose; and a direct comparison could be made with natural design in its striving for economy and efficiency by means of ingenious methods. But parallel to this, we can observe man's perpetual urge to decorate, to construct symbols, landmarks, and monuments — to expend almost endless resources, labor, and material toward ends we do not find in nature's design.

2   The Indigenous Builders

"The similarities between utopian and primitive societies are not based solely on the fact that they reside outside history. Primitive society (or our idea of it) is, to a certain extent, a projection of our desires and dreams . . . The future world of Harmony will be closer to the simplicity and innocence of the barbarians than to the corrupt customs of civilized societies."
— Octavio Paz, quoting Fourier[6]

BETWEEN 1948 and 1967 Jerusalem was divided by concrete walls and barbed wire, with little movement of people between the two sides, other than United Nations observers and other diplomats. For twenty-odd years two cultures existed, physically juxtaposed but totally separate from each other. In 1967, after the Six Day War, the city was reunited, and I became involved as an architect in some of its reconstruction.

One of the first things I did was to travel from Jerusalem, the Israeli side, to the eastern side, the Walled City, and onward to Bethlehem, Hebron, and Jericho. Suddenly this other world that had been hidden was revealed. I looked at it as one who had been assigned the task of building a new community in Jerusalem, asking myself what the environment for such a community ought to be. As I traveled south, I visited a settlement near Bethlehem that had been built after 1948 by Palestinian refugees. They had put up buildings that were quite minimal. They used stone and concrete block and tin roofs, but I was overwhelmed by the wholesomeness of the environment they had created. In twenty years they had built houses, created alleys and courts, and planted trees and vines. Both their private domain (within the houses) and the public domain (the village square) expressed a sense of wholeness. They had adapted themselves to the site, which was hilly, and they had done it with minimal resources.

In the same period of time — the same twenty years — tens of thousands of immigrants were settled by the Israeli Ministry of Housing in Jerusalem. The Ministry hired the best architects available and was proud of the multidisciplinary team of sociologists, geographers, and economists that had participated in the design process. Yet this team built horrible, anonymous, scaleless four- and five-story structures that cut brutally into the hills of Jerusalem. Some eight-story-high buildings were built with entrance bridges at mid-level on the side of the hill, so that they needed no elevators.

Here were two communities, each built at the same time, and two housing solutions. On one side there was a group of people, untrained and uneducated, who were dealing successfully by themselves with an environmental problem that directly concerned them. On the other side, there was a professional group, highly trained and sophisticated, backed by a social-welfare system, and having all the best intentions in the world — and the result was an unacceptable environment. This posed a whole series of questions for me about the design process, questions that for many in our generation have become important issues.

At about this time Bernard Rudofsky's exhibition *Architecture Without Architects*[7] was shown at the Museum of Modern Art in New York. It consisted of pictures of villages and towns that I considered to be some of the most exciting places I knew. As Rudofsky made very clear in his title, the towns were constructed without professional designers, and, indeed, they appeared to be more responsive to their environment than anything we had accomplished in the design profession.

As a student I had become aware that ancient Athens was not composed of a host of little Parthenons but in reality consisted of the Acropolis, surrounded by a world of indigenous architecture — houses that were more like the Mykonos and Santorini of today than they were like the Parthenon. Rudofsky's assertion that this architecture, this environment, which seemed to respond to people's physical and psychic needs and yet to embody the exactness and sophistication of design in nature, was created without professional input was overwhelming in its implications.

Much of my travel thereafter was to places where I could study some of these environments: to China's indigenous villages dug into the earth, to villages and towns in the Middle East, and to Indian pueblos in the southwestern United States. But the country that illuminated the potential of indigenous building for me, in both a rural and urban context, was Iran.

There I found a meaningful connection and similar spirit between the indigenous architecture of house and farm, fence and barn, and

Two communities in Jerusalem. One was built by a group of untrained people, who were uneducated. The other was designed by a multidisciplinary, highly trained, professional group working for a bureaucracy in a country with an advanced social-welfare system.

Village in the Iranian desert. Each house demonstrates an ingenious response to materials and climate. Mud brick structures exhibit sophisticated engineering techniques that were obviously arrived at by trial and error. Domes and vaults enclose large spaces. The mosque is of similar construction but is more elaborate.

the formal architecture of the mosque, the palace, and the city. The sophistication and beauty of what they had achieved at both the macro and micro levels overwhelmed me. As visible from the air, the desert landscape is crisscrossed by elongated mounds of earth that represent waterworks; these carry water underground for miles and miles from the sources in the mountains. A shaft is dug into the earth, then a tunnel is extended horizontally until it reaches the next shaft, and so on.

At each village there are stairs going down into the earth to allow the water to be collected, and above them are two or three enormous towers that jut above the skyline; these are louvered at the top and face the prevailing wind, with a large domed structure between them. This is the point at which the water arrives. The reservoir under the dome collects the water, while the towers capture the wind, ventilate the air over the water, and keep it cool.

In the villages of Iran, each house is a masterpiece of balance between material and climate. Mud brick structures exhibit sophisticated engineering techniques that are obviously arrived at by trial and error: These include domes and vaults and even double-barrel vaults enclosing large spaces. The mosque is of similar construction but is more elaborate: The brick work is more intricate, colored tile is used on the domes instead of plain tile, the domes are larger, and the vaults are more elaborate, yet it is constructed in the same spirit.

I remember a very interesting discussion with my friend Nader Ardalan, author of *The Sense of Unity*.[8] He said that the dome was very important to Islamic architecture because it was a symbol of the unity of the macrocosm, and that Moslems utilized the dome for its symbolic value. My own view was that the dome had evolved as a result of people building in a region that had no wood. With only small stones or mud bricks available, the only way to span a large room is via vaults or domes. Thus the dome was a response to the need to enclose large spaces with brick.

Nader claimed that I was too Darwinian in my interpretation and

Top left:
Wall defining and protecting an orchard garden in the desert.

Bottom left:
Simple farmhouse in the eastern Iranian desert.

Right:
Ventilators on houses in a desert village. Each house has a mud brick tower constructed so as to face the prevailing winds. The wind is captured by the ventilators and forced downward into a chamber that is kept damp. That air, which is at least fifteen degrees cooler than the outside air temperature, is then forced into the rooms.

Domes in the Friday Mosque, Isfahan. Did the dome evolve as a way of enclosing large spaces with small stones or bricks in places where wood beams were scarce, or did it evolve as a response to religious needs (because the dome became a religious symbol)?

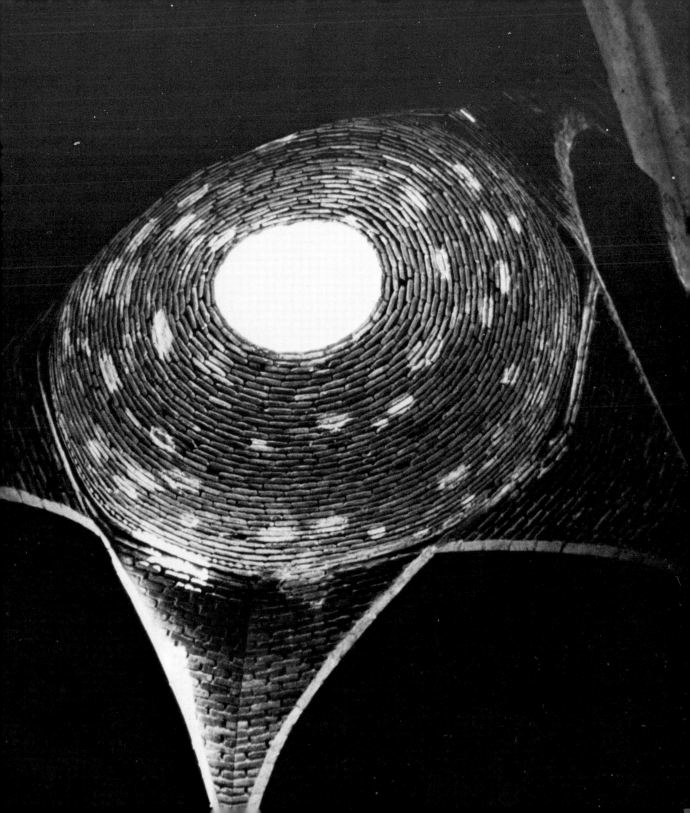

that it is for a spiritual reason that man has come to use the dome. After my discussion with him, I came to believe that both answers are probably correct. As it appears in Genesis, "And God said, Let there be light: and there was light. And God saw the Light, that it was good." Having built the dome, man observed and saw that it was good. And when he made a house and then a mosque, he made an even finer and greater dome — not only because it was an efficient way to enclose space with bricks, but because it had a sense of space and unity that transcended shelter, that bespoke of communion and worship of God. It was not either/or; it was both. But first there was the straightforward, unpretentious, unselfconscious act of a group of people trying to cover a big room with little bricks.

In the villages, each house has its own tower made of fine brick work, with louvers at the top facing the wind, to catch the air, bring it down through a place that is kept damp, and then force it into the room at a temperature fifteen degrees cooler than the outside air. All these towers form an almost unbelievable landscape, a collective jutting into the sky that is both symbolic and functional, combining form and purpose.

Because the desert is unfriendly, each cultivated plot, orchard, and garden is protected by a wall. The system of walls becomes a system for defining first each house, then the village, and, as one proceeds further out from the center, the entire network of canals and water-works.

Ingenuity extends to every component of the environment. As I drove from Isfahan toward the eastern desert, I passed a number of enormous mud brick cylinders that were about forty feet in diameter and five or six stories high. The only hint that there was something more to them was that they contained rather elaborate brick structures on the roofs that resembled vents. I was traveling with two Iranian architecture students, and they asked if I would like to visit the inside of one of these cylinders. They explained that the area was a fertilizer factory, built in the fifteenth century when Isfahan had grown and the region could not supply enough food for the city anymore. They needed a fertilizer to increase farm production, and chose pigeons as a solution. These structures, then, were built for the pigeons and designed in such a way that the droppings from all the nests collected at the bottom. I have been to Chartres, Notre Dame, and the Forbidden City in Peking, but this place, alive with light, with its intricate double and triple vaults rising all the way to the top, and with individual brick elements that form a nest for each pair of pigeons, has a visual and spatial impact equal to the greatest architecture I've seen.

I was convinced that the people who built the pigeon towers had no pretensions. They were simply trying to use available materials as effectively as possible ("effectively" in the Darwinian sense of the word), to make a place for pigeons. In doing so, they developed a cylindrical form with many-tiered arches that were arranged in a spiral fashion to support the domed roof structure. In other times and cultures, spatial impact was achieved only with a great deal of consciousness and sophistication. Discovering this wonderful example in the middle of the desert was indeed heartening.

I am convinced of the value of unpretentious, direct attempts to create an environment that responds to men's needs; of becoming attuned to the materials and processes available and using them in the most effective and efficient way. Any indigenous architecture must involve trial and error and refinement. How else can one explain the sophisticated solutions that are achieved? Without a knowledge of engineering analysis, it is hard to imagine how some of the intricate, three-dimensional mud brick structures could have been achieved, but it must have taken a very long time to develop these building types and forms. This continuous striving for perfection and for incremental improvement is analogous to evolution in nature. A change from one generation to another was not a stylistic change, a change of fashion, or a search for novelty — it was a constant attempt to improve what had been done previously.

Pigeon towers were built in the fifteenth century when Isfahan had grown and the region could no longer supply food to meet the requirements of the city. The structures were designed in such a way that the droppings from all the nests collected at the bottom.

This place, alive with light — its
intricate double and triple vaults
rising all the way to the top, with
individual brick elements that
form the nest — has a visual and
spatial impact equal to the greatest architecture.

Detail of the dome of a mosque. In the case of important buildings, colored, glazed ceramic tiles, as well as the application of patterns and texture, enhanced the sense of ceremony.

As these forms developed, the indigenous builders became adept at using them for a full range of social activities. In the case of important buildings — the mosque or palace, for example — the use of colored, glazed ceramic tiles, as well as the application of patterns and texture, enhanced the sense of ceremony.

But it must have been a slow evolution. Did it proceed smoothly or did it come to a halt periodically, locked in a stalemate of tradition? We know that certain organisms in nature undergo enormous changes and then level off when they attain a certain level of achievement; their rate of change slows down, and what they attain becomes built into the culture as a tradition. It is important to remember that as each member of society deals with his own created environment he accepts its traditions, since he has no compulsion to depart from them simply for the sake of deviation or to distinguish himself from his society. This does not mean that he didn't make his window a little different in design, or that the carpet he wove wasn't unique in the context of a family of traditional designs.

In one of those villages, I remember coming upon an empty lot where a man was laying out the plan of his house on the ground. Working with the topography, he was outlining the walls and the rooms with a pot of chalk dust. By virtue of this personal and direct involvement, he gave his house uniqueness, despite his use of traditional techniques for its construction.

What does this teach us today? What can we learn from it that will help us to resolve our own environmental needs? Is what appears to be a gradual evolution toward perfection a process that we can achieve today? Instead of striving continuously for novelty and individuality or for personal style, should we be more concerned, as the villagers seemed to be, with the gradual improvement of the collective and personal environment?

This issue is strongly affected by who makes the design decisions in the course of building, and how the decisions are made. One feature of indigenous society is that the user is directly involved in creating

A simple house in a village. A window made by its owner — unique and different from any window in the village but nevertheless part of a vocabulary.

his own environment. If people have a direct say in determining where they live and how it is built (whether they do it with their own hands or not), do they achieve a greater responsiveness to the environment? Surely the comparison between the Ministry of Housing and the Arab refugee settlement emphasizes the difference between, in one case, a bureaucracy's deciding what is good for people and, in the other, the people deciding for themselves.

What contributions have the more sophisticated contemporary builders, who are trained to treat design as a personal art, made toward achieving a wholesome environment? Is it possible that their concerns could ever contribute to the environment in the way the peasants' concerns do? This leads to the issue of fashion, novelty, and art, and to that of art in relation to artifact — the idea of the craftsman as distinct from the artist.

We know that some craftsmen excelled and were recognized for their excellence. As people came to build great edifices such as the mosques in Isfahan, great craftsmen were sought out, as must always have been the case when kings and priests built great monuments. When Darius built Persepolis, he searched for the great artists or craftsmen and commissioned them to carve the story of the kingdom.

What is important to recognize is that the quality and richness of the environment was the sum of the efforts of many people. If we attach the label "artist" to those who did the more complex work, then we can say that the artists of that age were directly involved with creating the environment. Their contribution was direct and integrated; the window was a better window and the door a better door because a skilled artist participated in constructing it. This is not the case today. Today, most of the effort of those who call themselves artists has no direct impact whatsoever on our environment. The fact that Picasso painted thousands of paintings has little to do with the quality of life in our cities or houses. The fact that sculptors make hundreds of pieces of sculpture, some of which are placed in our rooms or our gardens and piazzas, has little to do with the quality of these rooms or gardens or cities. Though artists may be the most

I came upon an empty lot where a man was laying out the plan of his house on the ground. Working with the topography, he was outlining the walls and the rooms with a pot of chalk dust. By virtue of this personal and direct involvement, the house will meet his needs and also have a sense of uniqueness.

gifted members of society, we have isolated them (or they have isolated themselves) from the process of creating the environment. When I asked the New York artist Christo to suggest a way of darkening the tent at the International Design Conference at Aspen, so that slides and movies could be shown during the day, he replied, in the tone characteristic of the attitude of so many artists today, "As much as I would love to meet with you in other circumstances, I do not work at anything practical and would therefore not be at all the right person."

In addition to the path of evolution within a culture, there is also a greater evolutionary process, which is cross-cultural and develops from culture to culture and from one period to another. We know that the Egyptians evolved building forms that were a touchstone for the Greeks. The Greeks evolved a vocabulary of building that was adapted by the Romans. There were, moreover, important technological developments at each step. For example, the Romans used the arch and the dome, which were not familiar to the Greeks.

One part of the world, then, might reach a certain level of sophistication that was beyond that of another part. What was happening in the Far East, for example, might not exactly coincide with what was happening in America at that time. Yet it is fascinating to discover that the most fundamental building types — the house and the village — have much in common in all cultures, even those cultures that were geographically isolated. The fact that a house in Yucatan, with a thatched roof and curved walls, corresponds so closely to a house in India, where there is a similar climate and similar building materials, is a convincing demonstration that what evolved was not arbitrary. It is almost like the similarity between the nests of certain birds in America and in Europe, or the fact that ants make their houses of mud, and bees make theirs of wax, regardless of what region of the world they evolved in.

In the Middle Ages we find, first in Romanesque and then in Gothic buildings, a translation of the same stone construction that the Romans used to create their aqueducts, baths, palaces, and markets: It is merely another realm of building technology and a new way of counteracting gravity that results in new dimensions of space and light. There are also new concepts of urbanism and new responses to the problems of defense. The technology and process of building were in a state of constant evolution.

It seems that this development process evolved until the time of the Renaissance. In the Age of Enlightenment and Reason, while new ideas burgeoned in every realm, the Renaissance builders adopted the building vocabulary of a civilization that had been extinguished a thousand years earlier. It is as if today we were to revert to the Middle Ages, assume the vocabulary of that period as the answer to our building problems, and build henceforth only in that one style.

As James Marston Fitch put it,

When Renaissance architects rejected late Gothic forms in favor of those of classic antiquity, they ruptured the seamless fabric of a thousand years of evolutionary development in architecture. And in the 400 years between Brunelleschi's *Ospedale dei Innocenti* and Jefferson's campus at Charlottesville, the Western world had no system of expression, no syntax of ornament and iconography other than those which derived ultimately from classical antiquity.[9]

The Renaissance architects expended enormous effort in manipulating these building forms into every conceivable combination, in order to meet the functional needs of buildings and cities. Natural evolution had been disrupted. What had been a historic progression was suddenly replaced by self-conscious manipulation of the vocabulary and formal elements of the classical orders, which were treated in a totally intellectual way and were quite detached from the problem of providing shelter. The Renaissance architects made a conscious and intellectual choice among certain building elements, to achieve an effect that was detached from any foundation in building technology or any response to living necessities. They turned their backs on the achievements of their immediate predecessors; they looked down on medieval architecture.

One of the qualities of indigenous environments is that the sum of the parts is greater than the individual pieces. For example, in desert villages houses are extended over the walkways, so that the street is shaded, thereby contributing to the quality of the collective space. In the same way, the houses define the edges of the public "room" that constitutes the market square. And because the vocabulary of forms is complementary, in the end the walls and entrances and roofs combine visually and spatially, just as a symphony combines individual passages and instruments. This principle seems to define the very nature of urbanism; a city or village is not simply a haphazard collection of people working and living independently but represents people converging, so that what each does as an individual contributes to a greater whole. Why were other cultures so successful at this, while, by comparison, we continually fail?

Seven houses grouped around a square or around a well create a space that is of greater importance than the individual space of each, and the unity of material and harmony of the forms give it a sense of place. Each house may have complete identity as a house, but if it has no connection to the houses around it, or no way of joining its neighbors, then it will not form a street or city square.

City squares are the living rooms of the city, and the conception of each individual structure involves the manner in which it joins others to form the rooms of the city. This interconnection is an integral part of city form. It is difficult to think of indigenous architecture in terms of individual buildings — often a line can't even be drawn between one building and the next. If you look at pictures of the same village taken in 1890, 1910, and again in 1920, the pictures show changes. The village has grown up the hill or expanded down toward the water; fields have been added and some houses have been removed. Yet while such changes can be detected, the totality nevertheless seems to be the same at any given time. It is like an organism that grows and contracts and changes.

In the desert village the houses are positioned so as to shade the streets. While responding to the needs of the individual family, the house nevertheless makes a contribution to the collective environment.

Right:
City squares are the living rooms of the city. The conception of each individual structure involves the manner in which it joins others to form the rooms of the city. It is difficult to think of indigenous architecture in terms of individual buildings — often a line can't even be drawn between one building and the next.

New development in the desert in the Middle East. Thousands of years of evolution and tradition are ignored. These forms are unrelated to lifestyle, climate, or site.

When I designed my thesis that led to Habitat, I realized that I couldn't call the project a building. I remember being totally confused about what to call it. In the end I called it "a three-dimensional housing system." Maybe I thought at the time that I meant a construction system — an assembly of hardware parts that can be put together to make houses. But as my thoughts evolved, I became aware that the word *system* has much wider implications, which relate to non-finite building.

I designed Habitat to cover the entire peninsula of Cité du Harve, but when it was decided to construct only a part of the design, it was not a question of building an incomplete structure (five out of twenty-five buildings); it was merely that the organism had shrunk and would perhaps grow again later. In Habitat the components draw back to form gardens; they are grouped into streets or come together around an elevator; they are eliminated in order to create a playground; they group as an assembly of parts to create a public place for shopping.

This is the point at which I realized that indigenous building is, in essence, an environmental system that is composed of components, wherein the collective is as important as the individual. It is an environment that is not finite but that forms a fabric. This is quite different from the attitude toward architecture that predominates in our own time — that architecture is composed of single buildings, each one representing an object in space, with its own *raison d'être,* which very often does not relate to what is around it. The idea that connection to an adjoining unit is as important as the unit itself is quite foreign to modern architecture. The commitment to urbanism by the founders of the Modern movement has become the subject of revisionism in recent years. Now, theories and attitudes do not emanate from a concern about the whole — that is, the city and its parts, the individual buildings — but rather see the building as an opportunity for a statement, by definition detached from its surroundings. Christopher Alexander and Serge Chermayeff resisted these trends when they entitled their book, written in the late sixties, *Community and Privacy.*[10] Not just "Privacy," or "Community," but a balance between community and privacy. The collective and the individual, one might add.

One of the things that I have always felt to be unappreciated concerning Habitat is its radical departure from Le Corbusier's "Unité d'Habitation," where several hundred families live in a massive block that is isolated in its landscape and embodies no notion of urbanism, continuity, or street life. Le Corbusier painted the balconies different colors in order to give some individual expression to each dwelling, but this served only to demonstrate the shortcomings of the beehive-like fabric. Bees do not need to distinguish one cell from another, but humans do, and this is demonstrated in one indigenous village after another.

The additive nature of indigenous building allows it to spread to accommodate streams, hills, groves, and fields. Because of their responsiveness and flexibility, the components adapt themselves to the topography and the particular features of the locale. Formal, high-rise structures and Houston-like sprawl of packaged buildings and roads, on the other hand, rape the landscape and cannot respond to the uniqueness of the site. This is why we have trouble achieving identity in contemporary housing projects. This architecture superimposes an abstract order that destroys the sense of location and creates a need for labels and signs. In its ability to interact with the land and the uniqueness of place, indigenous building demonstrates its superiority over a formalistic order.

3 The Sophisticated Builders

"The architect's power to formulate has caused him at times in the past to be deified as was Imhotep, the designer of the first surviving pyramid, and Michelangelo, who was called 'divino.' The very term *creativity* was first applied to artistic conception in the Renaissance to suggest a parallel to God's creation. Since the Renaissance, the architect often has been celebrated not as the member of the community charged with providing a shape to serve its needs and to convey its message but rather as an aesthetic shaman whose inventions might be visited upon a populace grateful for his fortuitous concessions to its wishes and hopes." — James S. Ackerman[11]

St. Peter's Cathedral, Rome.

EVERY TIME I revisit St. Peter's in Rome, one of the landmarks of the Renaissance, I am surprised to rediscover how unfulfilling and disappointing an experience it is. It lacks scale. Inside, its different materials and structural parts battle for prominence; its contrasting elements are out of proportion, and its sculpture is poorly integrated. Despite its size, the cathedral lacks a sense of wholeness or greatness. The bases of the columns are higher than a man, the molding is the size of a human body; the capitals do not adequately support the vaults and domes. Every element denies a clear sense of scale. Light penetrates poorly into the interior space, and there is no sense of how the weight of the great dome is carried down to the ground.

I visited St. Peter's first when I was fifteen, again at the ages of twenty-one and twenty-five, and then frequently thereafter. I always had the same reaction: It is poorly designed.

Like every other student of architecture, I have studied Renaissance buildings, the work of Brunelleschi and Alberti, and so on, and I've been educated to think of the great palazzi as landmarks in the development of architecture. But other than Brunelleschi and some of the early Renaissance builders, the architects of the period were prisoners of a situation that is incomprehensible, in view of the openness of thinking in science and other fields at that time. It is fascinating to read of their concerns about the proper relationship of the elements of classical architecture — the pediments and orders — all of which they regard as having intrinsic value. Yet their concern with proportion, balance, and composition seems strangely arid and detached from the problems of real life.

Having studied these palazzi in books, I traveled to Florence. In comparison to those in Siena and Assisi, the great medieval towns, the palazzi of Florence seemed to be caricatures. The structures start with stone rustication, surmounted by the piano nobile and other floors. There's a large central court but no sense of orientation, light, or response to the uniqueness of the site. Intellect dominates everything. The details speak for themselves: four stones joined to look like one, artificial joints that may be three inches wide.

Below:
Strozzi Palace, Florence. Side view as illustrated in Venturi's *Complexity and Contradiction in Architecture.* The contrast between the carefully composed windows on the street façade and the rather relaxed and complex placement of windows on the side of the building illustrates the conflict between "what the building wants to be" (to use Louis Kahn's phrase) and what someone has determined it should be.

Left:
Palazzo Strozzi, Florence. A formalistic order, dictating the position and size of fenestration, orientation, and building mass. The "normal" building on the left, which is designed to the scale of human beings, tells the whole story.

Courtyard of the Palazzo Pitti
by Ammanati (*below*) and the
courtyard of the Bargello
(*right*), both in Florence. The
medieval and Mannerist attitudes
toward the design of space, and
the extent to which different
building components and pro-
grammatic requirements are allowed to play a part in its formation, are apparent.

As time went by, the situation grew worse. Mannerism — the manipulation of building elements in a way that is totally detached from the direct purpose of the building or its logical construction system — came into vogue. For example, the Romans developed the pediment as a way of framing an opening in a masonry structure. But the Mannerist architect opened this pediment and pushed the keystone through as if it were floating in space. The pediment was then no longer a pediment. It was as if the architect were saying that the logical solution would be transformed instead into an object of surprise and shock by incorporating the unexpected.

Today, architects such as Robert Venturi have found in Mannerist and Baroque architecture a model for inspiration. Somehow the willful and tongue-in-cheek attitude predominates among many contemporary designers. The Mannerist architects pretended that an arch was not really an arch, and that gravity did not exist. They found new and clever ways to manipulate the classical order: Columns became twisted snakes, and stairs led nowhere. This was the architecture of effect. And, true to this tradition, we find in contemporary design a house in which there is a stair that leads nowhere and comes to a dead end.

During the Baroque period, architecture became a stage set. The Mannerists began by departing from the down-to-earth sensibility of the building process; the Baroque architect went a step further and declared that in seeking certain effects, all visual means and building elements — be they an integral part of construction or simply applied plaster, painting, sculpture, optical effect, or other deception — are legitimate ingredients. Compare, for example, two churches — a great Gothic church, such as Chartres, and a Baroque church, such as Vierzehnheiligen — which are both spaces built for worship in the same religion.

When I walk into Chartres Cathedral or Notre Dame or Salisbury, I am overwhelmed by the unique feeling of uplift, communion, and meditation, although I was not brought up as a Christian. On

New Year's Day of 1978 I visited Chartres during High Mass, while the organ was being played. There was a sense of place and of harmony with nature, of all elements working together toward a great spiritual experience. But why the sense of harmony with nature? I believe this is due to the attitude of the medieval master builder. The builders of Chartres wanted a great, soaring space. Pushing masonry construction to its limit, they achieved a delicate balance between the forces of gravity while creating the largest possible space, allowing light to penetrate into the church through the openings on all sides. The flying buttresses and the soaring arches — in fact, all details — contribute to that feeling. Every piece of sculpture is subordinated to the overall order. The sculpture is built in places where an "event" in construction is celebrated and is integrated into the vertical geometry of the façades.

The story of Christ and the Church depicted in the stained-glass windows is amplified by sunlight, so that light and color flood the space. And this natural light, with the sun appearing and then disappearing behind a cloud, creates changing moods within the overall space. Added to the richness of the music, the light imparts to the building a quality that is almost incomprehensible. Light, images, sculpture, color, stone, gravity, and music work together to uplift the spirit of the worshiper.

Now consider the Baroque church. On the surface, Gothic and Baroque churches have similar objectives. Many Baroque churches use sculpture and painting to achieve the illusion of weightlessness or of light. We are familiar with the extended rays of light, floating cherubs, and clouds painted on the domes, and the suspended plaster ceilings of Baroque churches. Compared with the Gothic, these effects appear to have been instituted to take the easy way out. Why bother with natural light, the sun, gravity, or any of these things? It is simpler to create an envelope, decorate it on the outside, and within that envelope create a stage set.

The stage set is synonymous with illusion. In the theatre, we know

Michelangelo. The vestibule
stairs in the Laurentian Library.

Above:
Giuio Romano. Ducal Palace, Mantua. As Mannerism evolved, every effort was made to disguise and manipulate traditional building elements. Once the building became the setting for freewheeling manipulation of forms, the way was open to treating architecture as a stage set.

Palazzo Spada, Rome. Detail of façade.

Left:
S. Michele, Rivarolo Canavese.
The Baroque: manipulation of
building elements in a way that
is totally detached from the
direct purpose of the building
or its logical construction system.

Right:
Chartres Cathedral, detail of the
transept. Pushing masonry construction to its limit, the medieval master builders achieved a
delicate balance between the
forces of gravity while creating
a great space and allowing light
to penetrate into the church
through the openings on all
sides. The flying buttresses and
the soaring arches — in fact, all
details — contribute to that
feeling.

Far right:
Pilgrimage Church of Vierzehnheiligen, interior view. B. Neu-
mann, 1744. Sculpture and
painting are used to achieve the
illusion of weightlessness, of
light and complexity. The result
is a sense of detachment from
reality — not merely a feeling of
illusion but the experience of
theatre.

that the set on the stage is not real, that the window and the wall are make-believe, and that the view beyond is painted for effect, rather than to offer a real view from the real world. We temporarily condition ourselves to an experience that, while meaningful, we realize is not reality. A similar impact occurs in the Baroque church. With the light painted on, as in the stage set, with stones and vaults only pigment, illusion must take over to achieve the effect. But the church is not temporary and the worshipers do not come there for a single event or experience. What works in the theatre because it is a singular experience rapidly deteriorates in the Baroque church, as routine visits demonstrate the static nature of the architecture and, in a sense, its detachment from reality. In the Gothic church, we have the feeling not only of being uplifted but that this experience is in unity with nature. We are, so to speak, nature's children. The light coming through the tracery is not unlike the rays of the sun filtering through a tall pine forest. In the Baroque church that sense of nature is denied us. The stage-set quality makes it an inferior experience with each further encounter, leaving us hanging, wanting to experience the real thing.

The contrast between pre- and post-Renaissance Italy offers much food for thought. It is interesting to compare the richness and complexity of Siena, Assisi, San Gimignano, and the medieval sections of Florence and Rome with some of the constructions of the late Renaissance and Baroque periods. Discussing these distinctions in academic circles is like attacking a sacred cow. Students today not only marvel at Palladio but, in designing a housing complex on New York's West Side, will literally paraphrase his work.

In his book *Complexity and Contradiction in Architecture,*[12] Robert Venturi analyzes in one photograph after another both Mannerist and Baroque buildings. He studies them in fine detail, discovering great subtleties, variations, ambiguities, and clever manipulation of space. The fascination with this period of architecture tells us something about the values and attitudes prevailing among architects today. We can gain greater insight into contemporary developments by understanding the forces that brought about the development of Mannerist and Baroque architecture.

In comparison to the Medieval period that preceded it, a fundamental, radical change took place in building during the Renaissance. Some of the differences are easily identified. For example, we do not know the names of the designers of the great Gothic churches — nor, in fact, of most of the designers of the great structures of earlier civilizations. We know that great craftsmen and artists were involved, but they rarely signed their work. (There also was no problem with continuity of style when one phased out and another came into prominence, although some buildings took several hundred years to complete.) In Germaine Greer's words,

Think of the crypt of a Romanesque church like Santa Maria della Pieve in Arezzo, where all the stone masons contributed their separate capitals to the columns. They are all wonderful. Brancusi would have given his eyes to have sculpted something as beautiful. But they're not signed.[13]

In the Renaissance, for the first time, the architect was identified as an individual. After studying Gothic architecture, we study Brunelleschi, Michelangelo, and Bernini. In other words, we study "architects." We stop talking about the generic issue of building and we discuss Palladio. To quote Greer again,

If you went back beyond the Renaissance and the emergence of individuals, you would arrive at a notion of art that was publicly useful — which produced sublime expressions of collective yearnings for something more perfect, like the Chartres Cathedral.[14]

What must it mean to live in a culture such as that of the Renaissance, where the efforts of an individual are personalized to such an extreme degree? That is easy for us to answer, because we live in a similar situation and are conditioned to it — indeed, we are totally intimidated by it. I am continually encouraged to create work that has a personal imprint. In like manner, the emphasis in Ayn Rand's *The Fountainhead*[15] (which is said to be modeled on Frank Lloyd Wright) is on the image of the great architect who evolves his own identifiable style as an expression of his person — not of his culture, community, or society.

With the advent of the Renaissance, the individual suddenly became the focus of attention, after generations of emphasis on the collective. This allowed the scientist to shed collective beliefs and theories in favor of an individual path of investigation that often challenged conventional wisdom. But the emergence of individuality contributed to the disruption of the evolution of building technology.

To quote Germaine Greer once again:

I think Western art itself is neurotic, wedded to the idea of the massive super personality. It is a Nietzschean and destructive notion and its most enormous function is to disqualify most people from understanding their own creative capabilities.[16]

Renaissance architects assumed an architectural vocabulary from the Romans and then found themselves facing more complex building problems. Two developments occurred. First, unlike the indigenous builders they did not try to resolve their formal and visual problems by starting from the roots of "what the building wants to be," to use Louis Kahn's words. Instead, the manipulation of formal elements and an intellectual approach to building took over. Second, the pressure to make a mark with one's own style — to innovate and to succumb to the demand for novelty — was so great that each architect tried to show how his work was unique. Hence we have the Mannerist architect and his continual search to outdo what had been done before.

Mannerism, however, grew not only out of the yearning for individual expression, but out of a sense of boredom. Architecture, having become the application of a formalized building vocabulary, no longer provided the tension and challenge builders had encoun-

Landmarks in the rural and urban environment. Village at Les Mechins, Quebec. Mosque in the city of Yazd.

tered when it was in continuous evolution. Playing around with this vocabulary, breaking the rules, became fair play. The same syndrome exists today. Architects, painters, sculptors, and citizens at large are conditioned by these attitudes. With the disruption of evolutionary development in building and in art, the new boredom emerges, and, once again, rule breaking becomes widespread.

Churches, museums, and government centers all represent symbolic gestures. The buildings serve the function of sheltering and serving what occurs within them but also have the function of announcing and celebrating their roles. Traveling through the Quebec countryside, one views the silver spires of the churches as marks that announce the villages from a distance. The minarets of mosques are similar landmarks in an urban fabric. In these examples no contradiction exists between the symbolic gesture and the function and purpose of the structure. In the Renaissance, however, the desire to express a symbolic gesture became so central that many aspects of livability were subordinated. For example, if for compositional reasons a façade with no opening on a certain floor was required, windows were omitted or tiny ones were constructed. The fact that the floor in question had the same need for large windows as the identical one below it was suppressed in the interest of composition.

Increasingly today, as a result of distorted value systems, we find architects allowing certain symbolic gestures at the expense of down-to-earth, straightforward livability. Consider the John Hancock building, I. M. Pei and Harry Cobb's sixty-story glass tower in Boston, a building that has had great impact and media exposure. Pei was engaged to design as the headquarters of a prominent insurance company a building that would house some eight thousand people who would work their eight, nine, or ten hours a day. The architect here was faced with two simultaneous demands. He had to create a space where these thousands of people could do their work, push paper, fill forms, attend meetings, eat their lunches, and go to the toilet; and he had to create a symbol for the John Hancock Company in the Boston

The John Hancock Tower, Boston.
I. M. Pei and Partners, Architects;
Harry Cobb, Design Partner. The
architect is faced with two simultaneous demands — to create a
place of work for thousands of
people and to create a symbol
that represents the image of the
John Hancock Company. Can
these objectives be complementary? Or are they contra-
dictory? What is the price paid
for a symbolic gesture?

Two perceptions of the same
building. The photograph on the
left was provided by the public-
relations office of the John Hancock Insurance Company. The
photograph on the right was
supplied by the architect's office.

Gorchev & Gorchev

cityscape — not unlike the position occupied by the church in the rural Quebec landscape.

The Pei and Cobb building is, in fact, a sparkling sculptural object that declares the presence of the John Hancock Company. Pei and Cobb's decision to clad the building with mirror glass, making it a glistening jewel that reflects its surroundings, is a clever solution and is an infinitely more effective building for this objective than is the honky-tonk Prudential Tower next door. But then we have to pause and ask what price has been paid in terms of quality of the environment and of livability. Has the architect given second place to the thousands of people who work in the building? Has he ignored, for example, the basic orientation issue that the north, south, east, and west faces of a sixty-story building should not each be treated the same way? That sitting next to a window on the south side is not the same as sitting on the north side? That the sun does not move evenly along the horizon and yet this building is the same on all sides? The Hancock building is a telling example of how contemporary architecture is prepared to pay an environmental price for a symbolic gesture — an unthinkable proposition for the indigenous builders of the past.

4　Art, Fashion, and Style

"In a truly normal society, the artist is not a special kind of man, but every man is a special kind of artist." — A. Coomaraswamy

". . . art and imagination are often taken as the 'frosting' to life rather than as the solid food. No wonder people think of 'art' in terms of its cognate, 'artificial,' or even consider it a luxury that slyly fools us, 'artifice.' " — Rollo May[17]

IN OSLO IN THE FALL of 1980, the theme of this book was presented to, and discussed by, the Aspen Board. The discussions touched upon many of the issues presented here. One evening, at a dinner given by our hosts Ulla and Alf Boa, we came to talk about art. At one point, Milton Glaser made a statement about the attributes of creativity. I asked him, "Milton, is the Turkoman weaving a carpet, who works within the framework of a tradition, not as creative as the contemporary artist you are talking about?"

Milton's first reaction was, "No, he is not. He does not exhibit the same kind of creativity we are talking about. He is not as inventive. He reproduces something that has already been developed."

This is a fundamental issue and the seed of a lot of misconceptions. Is the contemporary artist, who certainly does not have any allegiance to tradition, more creative? Is the carpet weaver less creative? In older cultures, art and craft generally were not differentiated. While the people who carved the reliefs at Persepolis must certainly have been recognized at the time for their excellence, they are not individually singled out today; critics don't analyze their art as a personal effort but rather as the output of their culture. Examining the wall-reliefs at Persepolis of the horses, parading figures, and lions all carved in stone, I imagined the artist going to the master mason, or maybe to the king himself, and saying, "I'm not going to carve horses and lions; I'm in my elephant period." The attitudes of the ancient Persian artist and an artist today are fundamentally different. But I don't think anyone would dare to say that the walls in Persepolis are lesser art than that of Rauschenberg or Paul Klee.

We can also observe in indigenous cultures that art and craft are integrated into architecture and the city, whether they involve weaving, embroidery, carpets, pottery, metal work, water pots, clothing, tents, or objects for worship. These are all made by craftsmen or by the people for themselves; they follow certain traditional patterns and contribute to the total environment. You cannot think of the architecture of a mosque without considering the carpets that cover its floor or the patterned tile work that lines its dome. They are inseparable. You cannot imagine the room of a Middle Eastern peasant without picturing the niches formed in the wall to accommodate utensils, or the embroidered bed cover that lends warmth, color, and texture to the room. You cannot picture a Japanese house, whose garden is a source of pleasure to those who live there, without recognizing the spatial relationship of indoors to outdoors. In these cultures the most creative people contributed directly to the enrichment of the environment, and the population as a whole could participate in the process.

At a certain point, sometime after the Middle Ages, the concept of the professional artist appeared. He emerged as someone who pursued an activity different from the activities of ordinary people. And because of that separation there were a number of changes. All of a sudden, for instance, the architect was not a builder; he was an artist, a master architect, who told masons and craftsmen what to do. He wrote books about his art and put his personal imprint on buildings. Historians began to write about his contribution.

As soon as artists are identified as individuals, an army of critics is needed to evaluate their work — and perhaps even to set a market value on it.

Later there was an even more alarming development. It can be argued that in the Renaissance, the architect, sculptor, and painter were still working closely together, and often were one person. Bernini, certainly, was a sculptor and an architect, and Michelangelo was all of these. But as we come closer to our own time, we find that this collaboration breaks down. The architect is distinct from the painter and the sculptor. From time to time, because the government decides that one percent of construction budgets should be devoted to art, the architect will commission an artist to do a mural or a sculpture that turns out to be totally unintegrated to the architecture. A piece of work is applied to the environment, yet it is cut off from that environment and is unrelated to it. Still, everybody seems to

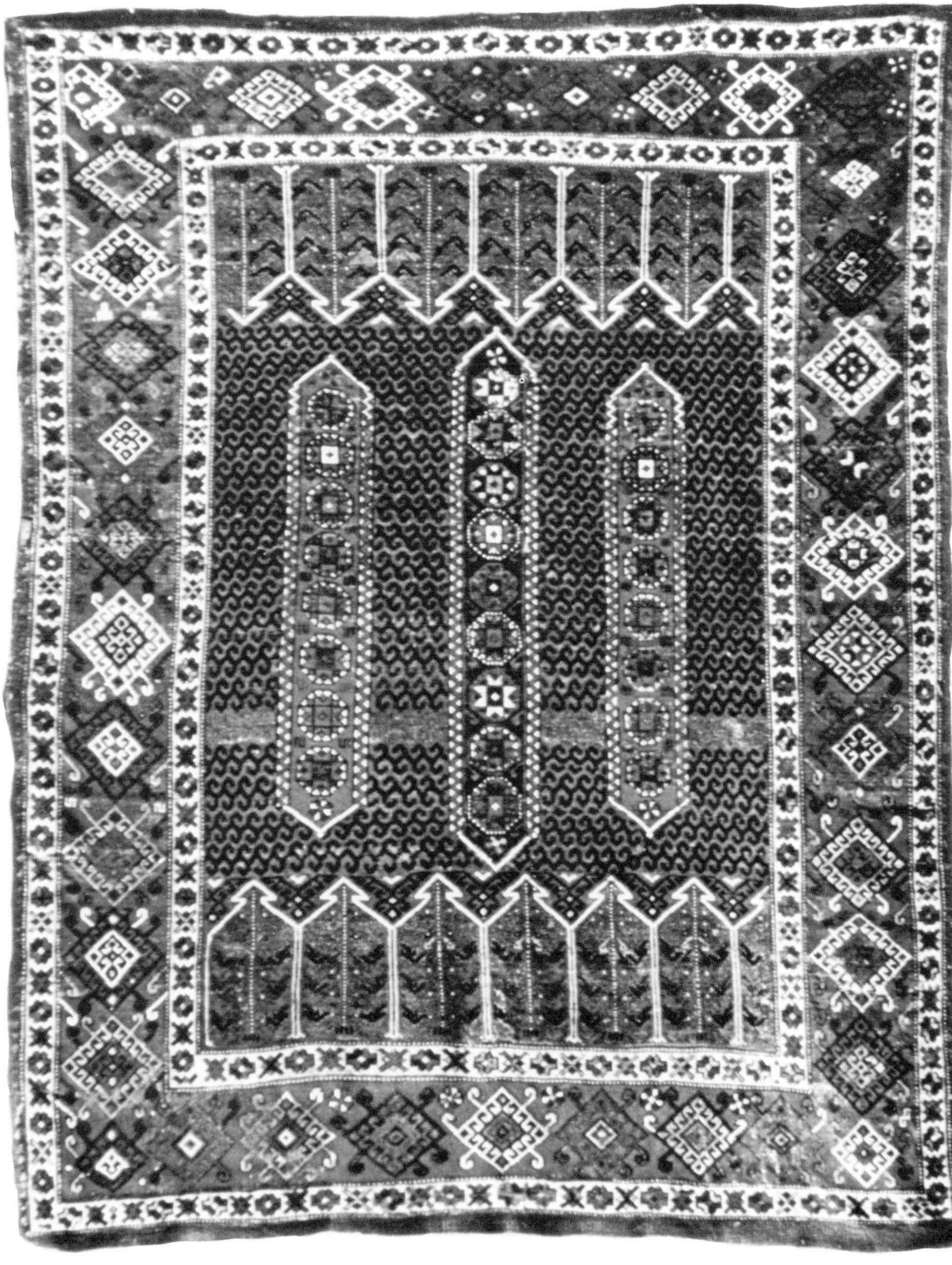

Persepolis. Stone relief, East Stairway of the Apadama, 700–600 B.C. Imagine the artist going to the master mason, or maybe to the king himself, and saying, "I'm not going to carve horses and lions anymore; I'm in my elephant period."

Right:
In indigenous cultures, art and craft are integrated into architecture. Weaving, embroidery, carpets, pottery, metalwork, clothing, and objects for worship are made by craftsmen or by the people for themselves, and contribute to the total environment.

Shokintei, Katsura Imperial
Villa. Integration of indoor and
outdoor space. The garden landscape becomes an essential in-
gredient of the environment. The
Japanese enrich the environment
with a garden, whereas we try
to do it by the application of art.

Rafael Ferrer, *Puerto Rican Sun*,
1979. Can art really make up
for the deficiencies we build
into our environment?

Left:
The Shah Mosque, Isfahan. One
cannot think of the architecture
of the mosque without considering the carpets that cover its
floors or the patterned tile work
that lines its domes. They are
inseparable.

Skylab's multiple docking adapter. Can you imagine NASA earmarking one percent of its budget for an art program?

view this development as acceptable — or inevitable. That separation between environment and art is a source of distortion, and a major cause of impoverishment in our lives.

Can you imagine NASA earmarking one percent of its budget for an art program? What possible contribution could an artist make to a space ship that is constructed with exactness, as a complete environment? This is as difficult to imagine as the thought of commissioning a work of modern art to be applied to a primitive mud brick mosque in the Nubian desert.

Now, I must make a very subjective statement, even though it leaves me feeling vulnerable. I have devoted a great deal of energy to understanding the environment and our visual world, and to cultivating visual skills. I know from my ability to synthesize form that I have the basic tools. And yet I have to confess that practically nothing that has been done in the name of art during my lifetime has had any significance for my understanding the universe: It is not a factor in how I conceive buildings. There are obviously some exceptions. But very rarely do I see evidence of the collaboration of various people, including artists, working in harmony to create our environment.

When I was designing the rabbinical college (Yeshiva) in Jerusalem, the rabbis said they wanted stained-glass windows in the synagogue. "Well," I said, "stained glass is a Christian concept. Stained glass means images, and the Scriptures say, 'He makes a graven image, and falls down before it' [Isaiah 44:15]." This argument did not impress the rabbis. They said, "Don't worry. Make them abstract." But I knew that stained-glass windows were out of place opposite the Western Wall in Jerusalem.

What did they really want? They wanted color, the sense of joy that colored glass gives. So I searched for a more fundamental way of achieving this, and from this search was born the idea of putting large prisms in the skylights. As the sunlight penetrated, it would break into the spectrum colors and flood the walls of the synagogue with color. Later I found an artist in New York — Charles Ross — who was working with prisms. He was very helpful in refining this proposal, building the prism, and studying how best to position it. Should there be three spectra or one? Should the bands of color be large or small? Should we break up spectrum pattern by putting in many little prisms? We worked together. We collaborated.

The Yeshiva in Jerusalem provides another example. One of its supporters is Stephen Shalom, who lives in New York. Shalom is a collector and appreciator of art, and as a member of the board of the Discount Bank of Israel he has been responsible for selecting a variety of works of art for display in the bank's lobbies and halls.

Traditionally, if you want something special in the way of furnishings for the synagogue — such as the ark, the pointers, the crown for the Torah (Scrolls), or the other ornaments — you look for very old items, such as from a fifteenth-century synagogue in Italy. There are wonderful examples in the Israel Museum. But Shalom told me, "When we build a synagogue, I would like some great artist to make these objects. We should have someone collaborate with you, so that the architecture and these objects which are part of the ritual are in harmony and so that they are as innovative as the architecture. We should have the artist make two exemplars — one for the synagogue and one to be placed in the Israel Museum." I was sympathetic to what he was saying, although I have to confess that my first reaction was, "I will design it myself." But my second reaction was, "It will be less rich if I do it myself." This notion that the architect does everything from the doorknob to the furniture, which Frank Lloyd Wright practiced by no means unsuccessfully, is not something one has to adhere to.

But I could not find anyone whose attitude and philosophy would make for creative collaboration and an integrated effort. The artists proposed to me were people who would view this as an opportunity for a highly personal expression that was unrelated to that synagogue, that place, or the uniqueness of that spot in Jerusalem. This kind of detached attitude exists everywhere today. Even when the artist is commissioned especially to do a particular door or mural in a certain room, he often sees this as another opportunity for personal expression and not as a responsibility to respond to the uniqueness of the place in a way that transcends his own self.

In fact, art and fashion are becoming indistinguishable. I think of art as an elevated activity that goes beyond the immediate, beyond particular personal idiosyncrasies, whereas fashion is a drive for novelty and differentness for its own sake. But increasingly the two are merging. It is almost impossible to draw the line between them, since the popularity of a single work of art now often has more to do with fashion, as determined by the critics and the opinion manipulators, than with art.

It has been fascinating to watch the emergence of pop art, and the seriousness with which it was taken. This movement was an almost embarrassing measure of the gullibility of our society. Pop painting itself was a protest movement, like Dada painting. Personally I can't consider either as art, and I am not alone. Lewis Mumford wrote recently: "The fashionable oppish and poppish forms of non-art today bear as much resemblance to . . . exuberant creativity . . . as the noise of a premeditated fart bears to a trumpet voluntary of Purcell."[18]

Pop and Dada were valuable as protests. Pop commented on the fact that throughout our lives we are bombarded by images — beautifully reproduced Campbell Soup cans on every billboard and in every magazine. But did people become more alert and sensitive to billboards in their environment? Did the protest register? Not at all. The public took it literally, as a serious form of art. Moreover, a whole generation of architects grew up taking it seriously, too, believing that the pop movement ought to extend into architecture.

It is one thing to protest with paintings, however, and quite another to protest with buildings that people are going to live in. To sacrifice a place in which people are to spend the rest of their lives — an edifice that has a hundred-year life span — is unacceptable and reckless irresponsibility toward those who live there. I find myself in

Claes Oldenburg, *Falling Fan, Model,* 1965. "The fashionable oppish and poppish art forms of non-art today bear as much resemblance to exuberant creativity . . . as the noise of a premeditated fart bears to a trumpet voluntary of Purcell" (Lewis Mumford).

Andy Warhol's *Soup Can,* 1964.

Jasper Johns, *Painted Bronze,* 1960.

Ellsworth Kelly, *Two Panels, Yellow and Black,* 1968. For the first time in history the majority of the population is uninterested and uninvolved in what artists are doing. This rejection is often expressed as, "Oh well, I could do that myself." What is really being said is, "I've learned nothing from it; it hasn't enriched me. I could have conceived it myself."

complete agreement with James Ackerman when he stresses the moral requirement for "a complementarity between the designer's power of free imagination and his responsibility toward the whole company of those affected by his invention."

The relation of the public at large to contemporary art is telling. Leaving aside the five percent that is sophisticated and sincerely likes the art, we are left with two groups. One group — the minority — is intimidated: It does not dare to say what it thinks or proclaim that the emperor has no clothes. Its members dare not pick what they like from a furniture store but must hire the decorator who did someone else's house, because they don't trust their own judgment.

The other group, which I believe is the majority, is not intimidated. It simply believes that contemporary art is meaningless. It rejects paintings of a white square within an off-white square, a pink circle within a green square. For the first time in history, the majority of the population is uninterested and uninvolved in what artists are doing. This rejection is often expressed as, "Oh well, I could do that myself." I am not saying that the man in the street has the skill to mix the acrylic paints and produce that subtle white square on another white square, but he knows that he could have conceived it. What he's really saying is, "I've learned nothing from it. It hasn't enriched me. I could have conceived it myself. It was not worth conceiving in the first place." As Gunther Stent observed in his book *The Coming of the Golden Age,* "Many people feel that art has somehow turned into a dead-end street and that for there to be *any* future an escape must be found from the present direction."[19]

In the past, the work of the craftsman was evaluated by the users. Those who excelled were recognized, and their reputation spread. The evaluation was direct. There was no intermediary. Today we have a profession that specializes in establishing the value of the work of artists.

Professor Karl Deutsch tells the story of a tomcat that stood by the window every spring and yelled his head off as the lady cats passed by.

The yelling became so loud and disturbing that his owner castrated him. Next spring came and there he was again by the window, meowing his head off. So his owner asked him, "Tomcat, now what are you yelling about?" And the tomcat said, "Now I want to go out there and be a critic."

Who are these intermediaries? They don't paint. They don't sculpt. They are not architects. Why do we need them to tell us that the work of this artist is good, and the work of that one bad? Why do three rave reviews of the work of a painter, and his support by an important gallery, double or triple or quadruple his value? Because we treat art as a commodity, an investment.

The human urge to collect is an ancient one. I collect artifacts of the cultures I work with and the places I visit. I collect kelims (woven carpets) from the Middle East. I find I get a better appreciation of some aspects of our environment from these kelims than I get from almost any work of art. Many of my friends are collectors, and their art is their pride. They like to have visitors walk through their houses and admire their paintings; they like to point out that one or another painting is a particularly good (or particularly early or particularly late) work by the artist. They never say, "Look at this painting. I am excited about this aspect of it; I got it because I was moved by it. I learned from it, it changed me." Instead they say: "It is a particularly good Pollock, an early Klee." They use critics' language, language that classifies. Maybe it is impossible to put our real feelings about a painting into words. Obviously if we could put into words everything we feel about a painting, we might as well write and not paint — or, for that matter, we might compose music. Still, the position of the critic as the tastemaker and manipulator of opinions is one of the most embarrassing things about our culture.

In a recent series of articles in the *New York Review of Books,* H. B. Allsopp traced the origins of art collecting. He showed how collecting emerged simultaneously with the concept of the individual artist, at the same time the monarchs began to regard the output of

Tracking a Trend
Prices of Fine Paintings, Mostly on the Rise In Recent Decades, Occasionally Can Tumble

By Roger Ricklefs
Staff Reporter of The Wall Street Journal

"The highest price ever for an American painting." "A record auction price for a Mondrian." "The most ever paid for a pre-Columbian work of art." As eager bidders shatter price records week after week, it seems that buying art is one game you just can't lose.

But how has art fared over a long period of time? A look at the record shows that art prices in general have climbed sharply in this century and soared in the last 25 years. But the important question is, which art? While many once-neglected painters multiply in value, some former heroes of the auction room sag. In art, even the "immortals" sometimes die. They merely take a while doing it.

As the chart at the right shows, prices for the 19th Century Impressionist Camille Pissarro spent the first 50 years of this century meandering through modest figures. Today they sell for six-digit sums, 100 or 200 times their turn-of-the-century levels. In contrast, the 18th Century Scottish portraits of Sir Henry Raeburn—once considered a rival of Gainsborough—commanded as much as $151,000 in 1913. Today, they commonly sell for less than one-tenth that figure—in 1980 dollars.

The history of art is full of fads and fashions. According to Gerald Reitlinger's "The Economics of Taste," mid-Victorian Britain went through a craze for the "strenuous life" school of painting. This stressed nature in the raw, storm-swept islands and titles like "Could Blaws the Wind Frae East to West." Art buyers of the time also paid fat sums for "misery paintings" of life among the poor.

From 1925 until the late 1950s, an investment in the stock market outperformed an investment in art, the Rush index shows. At 165 in 1929, the index fell to 100 in 1930 and 50 in 1933. It didn't reach the 1925-level again until 1945. Paintings in the index didn't rise as steeply as stocks in the late 1920s, but they fell slightly less in the Depression.

In recent years, the art market has trounced Wall Street. Salomon Brothers, the New York securities concern, estimates that between 1968 and 1979, prices of old mas-

understood pictures with action, strong detail and bright colors tend to enjoy brisk demand, he adds. This is one reason that 17th Century Dutch and Flemish "genre" paintings, with their scenes from everyday life, sell well now, he says. A village scene by David Teniers the Younger sold in January for $230,000, some 16 times its price in 1965.

While many contemporary British portraits are generally in the doldrums, 18th Century British landscapes or group portraits emphasizing the setting fare much better. "These paintings reflect a way of life that

ART APPRECIATION?

TOP PRICES PAID FOR PAINTINGS BY TWO ARTISTS DURING THIS CENTURY
(IN THOUSANDS OF DOLLARS)

$300 $250 $200 $150 $100 $50

RAEBURN
PISSARRO

1900s 1910s 1920s 1930s 1940s 1950s *1960s *1970s

*average of top auction prices for each year

Source: Auction Records and Gerald Reitlinger

Your Money Matters
Some Tips on Collecting Art and Antiques; Prices on Most Pieces Aren't Exorbitant

By Roger Ricklefs
Staff Reporter of The Wall Street Journal

A Matisse painting for more than $1 million. A Tiffany lamp for $150,000 and an elegant paperweight for $96,000.

So it goes in the glamorous world of high-priced art and antiques, where even a well-carved cigar-store Indian may command $23,000. But while a few sensational sales grab headlines, quality art and antiques can be far more affordable than many realize. At Sotheby Parke Bernet Inc., New York, the nation's largest auction house, 84% of all objects sold in the year ended last June 30 traded for less than $1,000.

A few of the rarest, most important Picasso prints do indeed sell for tens of thousands of dollars. But at one Parke Bernet auction recently, $1,000 or less would have bought lesser, yet genuine, prints by Picasso — and by Matisse, Klee, Whistler, Miro and Chagall as well. Quality contemporary prints by talented young artists are widely available for $200, says Milton Esterow, editor of Art News magazine. Most fine photographs sell for less than $1,000.

Many pieces of Victorian furniture cost less than their modern equivalents and may be better made to boot. Even some decent but simple 18th Century pieces are available at moderate prices. For instance, $750 recently would have bought an American Sheraton drop-leaf table, and $600 would have carried home a Georgian silver teapot, says Richard H. Rush, editorial director of the Art Investment Report, a newsletter.

To many, the market in art and antiques seems hopelessly incomprehensible. This is a world where a late 19th Century Humpty Dumpty mechanical bank can cost as much

Buying & Borrowing

Here are some recent figures on financial trends affecting consumers and individual investors.

—DOW JONES INDUSTRIALS—
Closing: 878.58. Year earlier: 865.82.

—MOODY'S CORPORATE YIELDS—
Average for Aa-rated bonds:
Sept. 27: 9.83%. Year earlier: 8.96%

—FEDERAL RESERVE—
Average bank rate on consumer loans:
August: 13.86%. Year earlier: 13.48%.

—FEDERAL HOME LOAN BANK—
Average effective conventional mortgage rate on new homes:
August: 11.02%. Year earlier: 9.70%.
Average price on new homes:
August: $80,700. Year earlier: $63,600.

In making purchases, experienced collectors tend to use both dealers and auction houses. Auction houses commonly charge 10% to both buyer and seller while dealer markups range from 20% or 30% to 100% or more. Though it tends to cost more to buy through a dealer than through an auction house, it is also more convenient and leisurely. Dealers generally will spend more time advising collectors.

Because any artist's work varies widely in quality, importance and physical condition, experts say collectors should mainly consider the worth of an individual work. "The classic mistake is to start by buying names alone," says Mr. Sogdon of Christie's. Parke Bernet's Mr. Redden says that as an investment, "a quality work by a lesser name is usually a better purchase than a second-rate work by a big name."

given artist in detail. Simply checking the watermark of an old print against the catalogue description may uncover a fake.

But the "keys to avoiding fakes are to deal with reputable people and to know the field," says Art News's Mr. Esterow. Sadly enough, this tends to rule out big bargains. The competent dealer who knows what he has also knows what it is worth. On the other hand, laymen rarely find spectacular bargains anyway, experts say.

The most prevalent trap in art isn't the fake, but the overpriced decorative piece that isn't worth looking at a year after year. As one collector points out, if art is worth owning, you can look at it time and time again and still find it satisfying. "People buy a very decorative print that they can relate to quickly, then find that after they have looked at it once or twice, they've gotten all there is to get out of it," he says. When they go to sell this type of work, they usually can't even recover their cost, he adds.

Even with the recent rise in art prices, profits are uncertain. One must buy retail and sell wholesale. Tastes change, too. The academic paintings by Meissonier and Bouguereau that smart collectors eagerly bought for $55,000 and $60,000 in 1890 now sell for $15,000 and $20,000—in today's money—Mr. Esterow says.

"Very few people make fortunes in art by consciously setting out to do so," the editor adds. Most experts advise collectors to buy what they like most and at least collect a dividend in enjoyment.

If the buyer has taste, buying for pleasure can be the best investment strategy too, experts say. The work that bores you may also bore the next buyer, they add. Mr.

artists as an investment, as part of the treasury. But as a major social activity and an extension of the stock market, buying a picture because it is a good investment (not because you enjoy it) is certainly unique to our time.

There is something astonishing about the way we have come to look to artists to correct our unsatisfying environment. In recent years we have built hundreds of city squares, plazas, and piazzas, and nearly every one is so desolate that cities have had to commission artists to do sculptures, to inject an element that was missing. The Richard J. Daley Plaza in Chicago is a prime example. Steel and glass towers rise straight up from ground level. There is no transition between building and ground where people can get shelter, no sense of the sun's penetration, no plant life, no animation or human use of that space. Is it for people? Is it a living room of the city? It is not. It is a dead piazza, a memorial to the corporation whose phallic tower dominates it. And so the city had to hire a great artist, Picasso, and commission him to make a sculpture. Three big sheets of steel. Three hundred thousand dollars.

There are two ways to look at this example. The first is to view it as an expression of a widespread attitude about the design of cities. Here we have a large public space in the middle of a great American city, surrounded by important buildings, and we seem to be so ignorant of what makes a place work that we have failed to give it even the minimal ingredients needed to transform it into a living room of the city. These ingredients include considerations of movement, comfort, microclimate, shelter from wind or rain, scale, and the need for certain activities. All we need to do is look at some of the great squares of Europe — Siena, San Marco, Piazza del Duomo — to get an idea of the elements required. But Chicago has the Richard J. Daley Plaza, which contains none of these things. And we have the cheek to call it a public piazza and give zoning bonuses to the developer for creating this barren land.

That is one side of the problem. The other side is the point of view

© Ezra Stoller

Far left:
Richard J. Daley Plaza, Chicago.
Sculpture by Pablo Picasso, circa
1965. The design of a public
square should involve considerations of movement of people,
comfort, microclimate, shelter
from wind, rain, or sun, scale,
activity, plant life, connection
and transitions to the surroundings. In the absence of these
qualities, can Picasso save the
day?

of the artist. In this instance we have Picasso, one of the great artists
of the twentieth century. He was asked to make a sculpture for an
important place in the city — in other words, he was asked to inter-
vene, to alter a part of the environment. One would anticipate that
as a creative man who cared for the environment and for people, he
would have found it unacceptable and immoral to get involved in
that kind of intervention, where all the basic decisions that made the
place good or bad for people had been removed from his control. One
might expect him to realize that in a place so grotesquely unsuitable
for people's needs, no one would be likely to appreciate what he had
to contribute. Nor would his creation affect the quality of life in the
square. Faced with this situation, he might have said, "Either I have
something to say about the conception of this place, and my sculpture
is an integrated part of people's experience of it, or I refuse to have
anything to do with it."

I have chosen Picasso as an example, but I could have picked almost any contemporary artist. Why do they sell out? Why is their
attitude toward their art so narcissistic, so egocentric, so detached
from society that they can do their work without caring about the
context?

It is not just the artist who should be questioned. This attitude is
a factor in the whole relationship and accountability of architect and
artist to society in our culture. It is difficult to blame people for latch-
ing on to art to improve a poor environment, when what we so often
produce in the way of space for people is inadequate. The only way
people know to enrich their surroundings is to turn to painting and
sculpture.

This is Art the Fixer — the anesthetic used by architects. Imagine
two offices. The first is a room that has on one side a glazed bay window, and there is a place for growing flowers. The room's walls are
of a material that is warm and rich in texture; there are wood beams;
the stucco and the wood trim interplay; there is a table, and books.
Contrast that with the office of someone working for a large corpora-

Faneuil Hall Marketplace, Boston. Benjamin Thompson, architect. No one has found it necessary to place a sculpture in the
center of this marketplace. Day
and night, it is alive with people.

Interior office, contained by modular partitions and ceilings. One has no sense of the movement of the sun or of weather changes, or whether it is day or night. One has to look at a watch to gain a sense of the passage of time. There is no repose for the eye, no change of focus, no view. The remedy is to hang a painting or poster on the wall.

tion, who is assigned a ten-by-fifteen-foot space in the innards of one of those huge office structures. Since he is not yet a vice-president, he hasn't made it to the window. There he is, contained by a modular partition for eight hours a day, in his ten-by-fifteen cell block. He has no sense of the movement of the sun, or of weather changes, or of whether it is light or dark. He needs to look at his watch to have a sense of the passage of time. There is no repose for his eye and no way to change focus by looking out to a view and then back to his papers. What is he to do? The first thing he does is to acquire some type of artwork. If he can't afford art, travel posters will do. He latches on to art to redeem the inhumanity of the place. But art cannot humanize what is inherently inhuman.

The richer the environment and the more fulfilling it is, the less dependent we are on artificial ways of improving it. One of the reasons for the current popularity of reproduction art (the supermarkets in both industrialized and developing countries are full of paintings for popular consumption) is the enormous amount of unacceptable space we create. When the environment lacks the richness and complexity we desire, we reach for something to improve it.

To reiterate, art and fashion, in our time, have become somehow almost indistinguishable. To quote Ackerman again,

If there was no paragon in the past and no definable goal in the future, criticism courted the danger that the only measure of the worth of a new work would be its newness, which meant that there would be no way of distinguishing meaningful innovation from faddism.[20]

Christopher Lasch echoes the same view:

Constant experimentation in the arts has created so much confusion about standards that the only surviving measure of excellence is novelty and shock value, which in a jaded time often resides in a work's sheer ugliness and banality.[21]

We create cycles of acceptance for art products just as we do for fashion. Both are influenced by manipulators of taste: In one case it

Above left:
Curtain wall architecture, circa
1950. (From a United States
Steel advertisement in the
Architectural Record.)

Above right:
Mirror architecture, circa 1970.
(From a PPG Industries advertisement in *Progressive Architecture.*)

Below left:
Yamasaki, Leinweber & Associates, Wayne State University
College of Education, Detroit,
1960.

Below right:
Edward Durell Stone, Gallery of
Modern Art, New York City,
1955.

is the critics; in the other it is Madison Avenue. Though the manipulators are not exactly the same people, they certainly appear in and
use the same media.

   Why should we expect the architect to be able to transcend all
that? The architect is part of the context. A good test is to see how
quickly buildings have become dated. Stand in the square in Siena.
You don't feel that after five hundred years these brown-colored
buildings have become dated; nor will they in another five hundred
years. You don't look at the Nash terraces in Regent's Park in London
and think, "Oh, they might have been good in 1820, but they're
passé now." But we walk around New York today, and lo and behold,
Lever House on Park Avenue, which was acclaimed when it was built
in 1952, is dated. There is talk of demolishing it.

   Some architects have transcended fashion. I have never felt that
there is anything dated about a building by Frank Lloyd Wright or
Louis Kahn. I do feel that something is dated about some of Le
Corbusier's buildings, but it is the concept — for example, the concept of Unité d'Habitation, the apartment block in its park setting.

   A walk through any American city is like an excursion through an
archaeological fashion catalogue. Beyond the traditional brick and
stone buildings are those blue and green glass-curtain walls that shout
"Nineteen-fifties." (Because they were built so badly, they are falling
apart and buckling.) Then, further along the block, bronze and glass
tell you that you are into the sixties, and after that there is the "sun-
glass" architecture of the seventies. It is like coming into a room
where everybody is wearing mirrored sunglasses. Belligerent?
Friendly? You don't know. Then we come into the late seventies
and, alas, the eighties — whimsical, eclectic, playful; joke architecture. The very fact that we feel that these buildings are dated
shows us how shallow, how unintegrated into the environment they
are. We also see the individual architect trying to identify himself by
his own personal style. In most cases the identifiable style is just a
visual gimmick, something tacked on for identification.

We are far enough now from the fifties to laugh at that decade. But have we forgotten how, in reaction to "the severity of modern architecture" (with its glass boxes and distortions) and the oversimplifications of Mies Van der Rohe, Edward Durell Stone mastered grille architecture and slapped grilles everywhere — even right onto the cover of *Time*? And then how Minoru Yamasaki, before erecting the two obelisks of the World Trade Center in New York, worked through every permutation and variation of intricate Gothic tracery, in the name of the architecture of delight, but did not quite make *Time*? Architects, not particularly gifted ones, made it with the media and the public, and were commissioned to do all the great buildings (the embassy in Delhi and one or another cultural center), because they were catering to some inner need to achieve an identifiable style that would be "in" for three or four years and then out the window. As for determining the value of these stylistic inventions, all you need to do is look at these buildings today. As Octavio Paz puts it,

Before and beyond history, North American society overvalues change and conceives of itself as the will to annex the future.[22]

What is fashion? Let us examine the sari as a form of dress. For hundreds of years the sari has persisted in India. It has evolved to meet the needs of women's dress, exhibiting regional variations and great richness and diversity in materials and colors. There are cotton saris, silk saris, and a whole tradition of designs. Great investments are made in saris. They are passed on from mother to daughter. I have friends in India who have a collection of saris going back three or four generations. They cherish them and wear them. The sari is adaptable to new conditions. Some saris are now made of synthetic fabrics, but they are still saris. The sari evolved as a response to a need, and then acquired a permanent place. There may be microvariations in fashion, but not macrovariations. The sari is the sari. You don't find Indian women suddenly appearing in miniskirts

For hundreds of years the sari has persisted in India. It has evolved to meet the needs of women's dress, exhibiting regional variations and great richness and diversity in materials and colors.

(although contemporary Indian teenagers are very happy to trade their saris for Western dress).

The sandal has a similar history. For hundreds of years, people have worn sandals. Despite minor variations in design, the basic form has persisted. But in modern Western society, fashions in women's footwear change constantly. The shoe tilts to sixty degrees from the horizontal; the entire weight of the wearer is brought down on a half-a-square-centimeter heel, penetrating through flooring and carpeting material, making it impossible to pave surfaces with anything but polished stone and terrazzo, and turning a floor grille into a dangerous obstacle.

People's toes stay the same, but suddenly the rounded shoe becomes pointed. The entire shoe is raised three or four inches off the ground, in a new heel-sole combination — platform shoes. Then open shoes are in, come winter, come summer. Then boots are in, and suddenly no matter how hot it is — or whether you live in Bombay or Boston — boots come up to the knee, go over the knee, go all the way up to the hip. So you get nakedness and concealment, pointed and rounded, raised and tilted. It is impossible that all these different forms respond to the comfort and walking needs of women. The foot, the leg, the whole physiology is distorted — and worse than that, women are allowing themselves to be manipulated, in order to meet some expectation, to be "in," to be up-to-date, to be à la mode. Is this phenomenon due to people's insecurity in exercising their own judgment, or is it due to something else?

Even more-grotesque distortions arise from people's insecurity in their own culture. In the Middle East, western Africa, and India, men still wear black suits, ties, and shirts even when they work in eighty- or ninety-degree heat and one-hundred-percent humidity. Insanity! I have been to bourgeois houses in Bombay where the floors were covered by wall-to-wall carpets and there was plush, upholstered, woolly furniture and an exorbitant investment in air conditioning, to keep the furniture from growing moldy. The tradi-

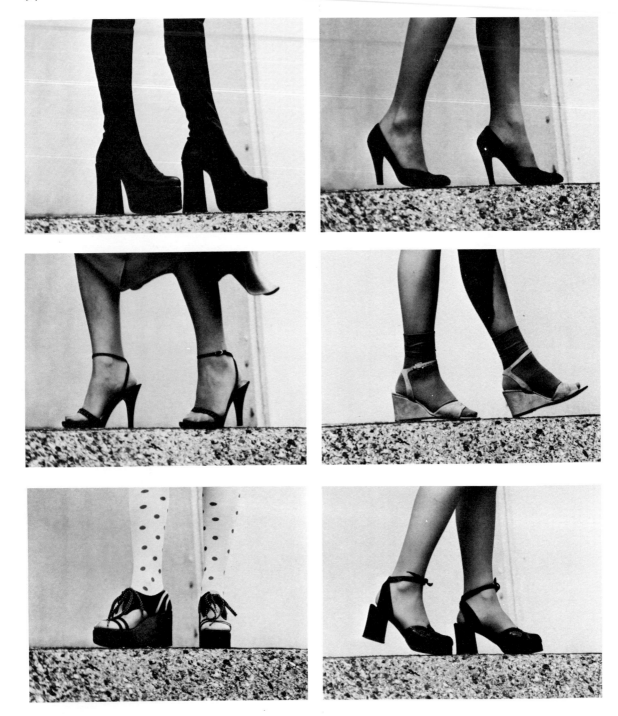

In a few decades, women's footwear has gone through endless transitions — pointed, rounded, at 20, 30, or 45 degrees. Weight is concentrated on half a square inch. Platforms, boots, and every other conceivable variation are found in the shoe, but the physiology of the woman's foot is a constant!

tional and sensible style in Bombay includes a tile or masonry floor; it is cool, and you can water it in the dry season and simply wipe it clean. Furniture should be of wood and straw, not of wool. We are continually manipulated. We perpetually strive to meet some abstract standard, and it is about time we rebelled.

It is not possible to talk about fashion without asking whether fashion is essentially the result of manipulation by our consumption-oriented economy, by those who want us to throw out our cars or dresses and get new ones, or is instead a response to a basic need of contemporary man for novelty and change. Obviously there is a difference between wearing the same traditional embroidered dress or form of clothing throughout one's lifetime and going through twenty-five cycles of change in taste, style, and form. While it is interesting to note in Bernard Rudofsky's penetrating book *Are Clothes Modern?* that grotesqueness and distortions are not unique to our time (the people of earlier times pierced and stretched their ears, tattooed their skins, scarred their legs, and plucked their eyebrows), it is also true that most of the historical examples in Rudofsky's book remained culturally constant from generation to generation.[23] The African tribes that mutilated their lips and ears, to hold jewelry, did not change that practice every two or three years. For modern man, fashion is the result of both influences. It probably does fulfill certain subtle needs, but by and large I think it is the result of manipulation. Even our frame of mind that expects and needs novelty is to some extent the result of brainwashing. I don't think we would expect to find this craving for change and newness unless we were continuously told to expect and indeed demand it.

The element of choice is something that we in the West claim to cherish. But fashion has made choice one of the big fallacies of our culture. Most people will tell you that one of the wonderful things about our society is the element of choice. But these same people buy the clothes that fashion makers design for them, and exchange them when fashion changes. Choice is continually eroded in a culture that

Piazza d'Italia, New Orleans.
Charles Moore, architect. Associated architects: Allen Eskew
and Malcolm Heard, Jr., of Perez
Associates, Inc., and Ron Filson.
Is architecture an acceptable
medium for making commentary? Is it meaningful to make
literal connections, such as eclectically reproducing an Italian
design in a stage-set way because
the building is in an Italian
neighborhood? The cynicism is
fully comprehended only when
this piazza is seen in the context
of the dilapidated streets that
lead into it.

is oriented toward rapidly changing fashion, and thus we have
conformity.

One of the questions an architect is often asked by laymen is,
"What style do you like?" or "What style is your architecture?" The
rabbis in Jerusalem believed they wanted a traditional building. They
had already fired two other architects, and when they hired me they
said, "Will you make for us a traditional or a modern building?" To
avoid the issue, I said, almost defensively, "If I succeed, when the
building is built you will not be able to answer that question."

People use the word *style* continually and in many contexts. It has
become a charged word. I would like to make a distinction between
two kinds of style. But first, we must recognize that there *is* such
a thing as a style. The combination of elements that is found in
Georgian architecture can be identified as a style. (At least we use
the word to identify that combination of elements.) We use the word
style to describe the formal, visual framework of an epoch or a culture. And we also use it to identify the work of an individual. Thus
we use the same word to describe two distinct spheres, two very different ideas.

I think there is a kind of style that is rooted in process and in the
components of building, and that has evolved to a level of common
acceptance. The key here is the word *process.* The Iranian desert
villages have a distinct style, one that is rooted in process — the mud
brick, the texture and forms that it generates in walls, vaults, and
domes, and in certain building elements like the ventilator and the
court enclosed by walls. The collection of details and components —
inclined roofs, eaves, frames, and stucco panels — in rural British
architecture or in Scandinavian architecture results in a style. When
it is part of that culture and built in conformity to a tradition, then
that is one thing. But when it is taken out of context and repeated in
a chalet built in a Mexico City suburb for a nouveau riche millionaire,
that is something else. Pulling style out of its native environment and
placing it in a foreign context constitutes an artificial act, a declaration of bankruptcy.

In our own culture we seem to be preoccupied with styles that are not rooted in process. There are exceptions: The glass office building is rooted in process, and constitutes a style. One can agree or disagree with it, but this combination of building elements is a style. The work of Mies van der Rohe possessed a style; in fact, it did much to set the style of a decade. Grotesque distortions were necessary to assemble the elements he used into a style. The very notion of a glass box as a neutral space is such a distortion of our needs that his style could only emerge at the expense of achieving a wholesome environment. But it was nonetheless a style. What came after it was not. We are told by Arthur Drexler that in 1960 Mies was asked how he spent his day. His reply was this: "I get up. I sit on the bed. I think, 'What the hell went wrong? We showed them what to do.' "[24]

Style is the result of an evolutionary process in which the methods and materials of building, on one hand, and the spatial organization responding to lifestyle, on the other, are synthesized and distilled into a building and urban vocabulary. Sometimes there is leapfrogging when an individual in a single lifetime contributes greatly to the development of style. Such was the case with Frank Lloyd Wright, who at the turn of the century first understood the far-reaching implications of the new building materials, of large glass surfaces, of the structural possibilities of concrete, and of the opportunities this created for the relationship between indoor and outdoor space and for the interweaving of a building and its site. But we must remember that Frank Lloyd Wright's contribution, notwithstanding his claims of invention, was built upon a heritage of which he was most conscious and appreciative.

But the search of each individual artist or architect to make his work unique — hence, to achieve a personal style — means that the key notions in modern architecture are individual expression and distinction: Edward Stone with his grilles, Yamasaki with his arches, and so on.

We should not use the word *style* unless we really mean something that arises from process and lifestyle. If we mean something else — a gimmick, a visual trick — it would be better to use some other word, perhaps the word *trademark.*

I was visiting with friends one evening, one of whom is a prominent physician and medical researcher at Harvard. In the course of the evening I said, "What I would really like to do is design a hospital. If I'm ever commissioned to design a hospital, I would leave everything and for six months I would live there." I said that no one had yet resolved the contradictions posed by the design of a hospital, and that that was why I wanted to do it.

He said, "I wonder what you mean. There are architects who specialize in hospitals, and they really have come up with some pretty efficient solutions to the functional problems." He explained these as ease of control from the nursing stations, the efficient flow of food and laundry, circulation, and so on. "I guess you're talking about making hospitals look a little better on the outside," he added.

The lay interpretation all too often revolves around fixing up the outside. I said, "Are you telling me that the function of a hospital is no more than the utilitarian flow of materials and goods? You've not said one word about what kind of a room or space the patient should have. You've said nothing about the environment of the tens of thousands of people who spend their lives working in a hospital, or what their needs are — the nurses, the cooks, the orderlies. You've said nothing about what a doctor needs to work efficiently. You've talked about the flow of food, but you've told us nothing about the *quality* of hospital food, which is a notorious joke. Isn't that part of the function of a hospital? You're not talking about function, you're talking about just an infinitesimal aspect of it. You degrade the architect if you think he's just concerned with facelifting and styling the outside. When I say I would like to design a hospital, I'm talking about a program that would involve the most intimate dialogue with those who manage, work in, and use the hospital."

I am sure that there must be innovative ways of transforming a hospital. Maybe the way the hospital room meets the needs of the patient transcends every other requirement, and perhaps one ought to start by questioning the scale and size of these places. I don't know the answer, but I do know that the meaning of the word *functional* was distorted in that conversation.

One often hears people say, "Well, it might be functional, but it isn't beautiful," or, more often, "It's a beautiful building, but it's not functional. It doesn't work." That is a contradiction, an impossibility, and I do not accept the basic assumption. That is not my understanding of beauty. We never use the word *beauty* that way in reference to nature. We never say that something in nature is functional but not beautiful, or beautiful but not functional. In the same way, people will say, "Now that you've solved the functional problems, what about the aesthetics?" You hear that every day. One percent for art; five percent for aesthetics. The very word *aesthetics* is a curse. When an interviewer asked Charles Eames, "Do you design for pleasure or for function?" Eames retorted, "Whoever said that pleasure is not functional?"[25] By function, people mean the most basic — indeed, base — elements of utility (and often not even all of them); and every other one of our needs is dismissed as vague, undefinable, or inexplicable, and generally subsumed by the word *aesthetics*.

When people say "aesthetics," they refer to some kind of need, or else they wouldn't talk about it. It is a shorthand way of referring to a whole set of feelings they have difficulty expressing. For convenience, and perhaps out of confusion, they set it apart from function. They don't see the interdependence of the two, and the need to expand the word *function* to include all human needs.

5 City Fabric

The probable result if land parcels were divided and different architects were assigned to undertake the design of individual buildings, without any attempt to establish common vocabulary guidelines.

THERE WAS A TIME when architecture and urbanism were inseparable, when concepts and actions of building always considered the private and public, accommodating an individual need in the context of the collective environment. The newly created schism between architecture and urban design poses a contemporary dilemma. Let's assume that a new university has been established. The administrators, being culturally aware, decide to canvass the learned members of society, to determine the great architects of the time. By this method of inquiry, they identify five important world-renowned architects — perhaps Kenzo Tange, James Stirling, Arthur Erickson, Oscar Niemeyer, and Philip Johnson. Let's assume that the selection is widely approved. These men are called together and told that the university intends to build a complete campus from scratch, at once.

It is absolutely guaranteed that if these five architects were commissioned to do the campus, they would not be able to reach any consensus about what to do. They would certainly be unable to design a group of buildings that had any sense of continuity or unity, to design a complex in which the individual buildings contributed to the greater ensemble, so that the whole was greater than the parts. They might choose one of their members and say, "Go ahead, you create the framework." But they probably would not let anyone take the lead and establish a framework to which the rest would have to subordinate themselves. They would be more likely to do what architects do all the time: that is, divide the pie, take a quadrangle or separate area, and each go his own way. The results would certainly not be Cambridge or Oxford. So how is it that the contribution of several individual architects over a period of time achieved in Cambridge a sum that is greater than its parts? And how is it that today we are unable to agree on any common denominators?

Those questions and others like them persuaded me to accept the invitation to head the urban-design program at Harvard. Through my work in Jerusalem — particularly the large-scale projects such as Mamilla and the Western Wall precinct, which will take twenty or

Niemeyer (1957); Bonaventure Hotel, Los Angeles, by John Portman and Associates (1976); Snyderman House, Fort Wayne, Indiana, by Michael Graves (1972); Nakagin Apartment Tower, Tokyo, by Kisho Kurokawa (1972).

thirty years to complete — I have become aware that the major problem is to find the framework, the common denominators. We must search for principles we can agree upon, so that several architects can work on different parts of a city and yet produce structures that are additive and contribute to the whole.

This conclusion leads to a much larger issue: that of the fabric of the city. Our built environment does not consist only of individual buildings: It *is* the city. Of course, the city is made up of individual buildings, uses, and functions, but what we desperately need is a wholesome and satisfying urban existence. We have become primarily an urban society. For the first time in history, over half of the world's population lives in urban areas. We spend as much time outside individual buildings, in the spaces of the city, as we do inside them. If we cannot create an environment in which the public domain is satisfying — indeed, enriching — then we have failed to meet society's needs.

Basic problems of the city — traffic and transportation, congestion and pollution — remain unresolved. But the objective is still to build the city out of parts that add up to a wholesome environment, notwithstanding the wave of utopian proposals and movements, garden cities, and projects such as Broadacres, Ville Radieuse, and the like. No region has a monopoly on this failure: The suburbs of Paris and Athens, new and old cities in America — Houston and St. Louis, for example — and cities and towns in developing countries, all fall short.

In almost all ancient cities, on the other hand, there seems to be a common thread, a collective unconscious at work. Consider Isfahan — particularly the Isfahan bazaar. It is as though a rule book that explains how to create a street, a square, a court, or how to cover an outdoor courtyard had guided every aspect of building. These conventions describe connections and establish the common vocabulary and the accepted grammar.

As was the case with indigenous buildings, which evolved through

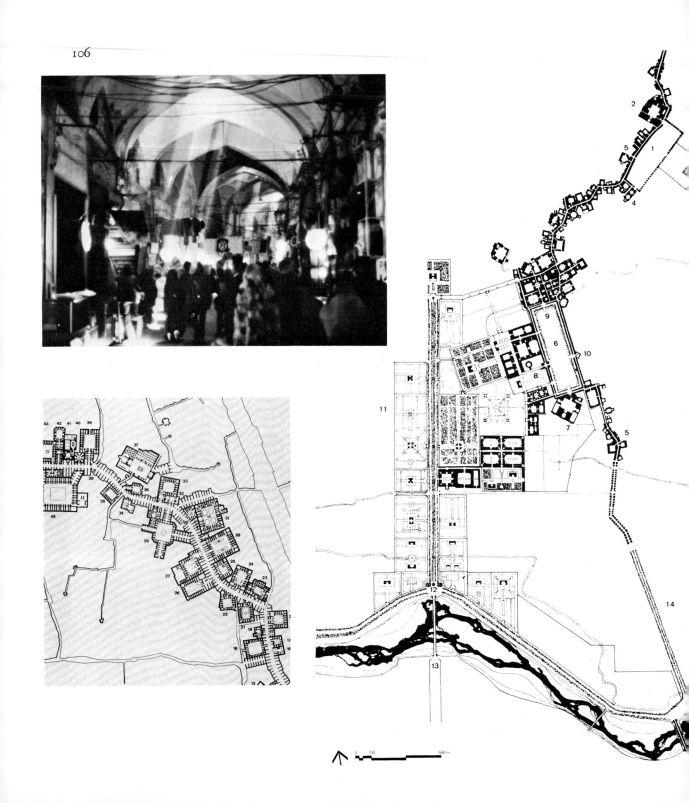

Above left:
The bazaar.

Right:
Plan of the Isfahan bazaar.
(From Nader Ardalan and Laleh
Bakhtiar's *Sense of Unity*.) The
bazaar as an institution makes
its demands on the design of
every adjoining structure. It
functions as a connector so that
the mosque, the school, the bath-
house, and the whole hierarchy
and network of public spaces —
linear or contained, covered or
open – can be plugged in.

Below left:
Plan of Isfahan bazaar, detail.

trial and error, so too, on the larger scale of the city, the public domain receives focused attention. The bazaar, as an institution, makes
its demands on the design of every adjoining piece of construction. It
functions as a connector, so that the mosque, the school, the bath-
house, and the whole hierarchy and network of public spaces —
linear or contained, covered or open — can be plugged in. It is like a
grammar that makes possible the writing of words and sentences —
and sometimes poetry.

The medieval European city has similar qualities, engendered by
the compactness that the needs of defense required, as well as the
clearly established hierarchy of public spaces for both secular and
religious activities. But there have been other ways in which the concept of city interacts with that of individual buildings. This is what
I call the compositional approach. Some examples are Bath, Georgian
London, and Haussmann's Paris. In these cities, the public spaces
were designed before the individual buildings. In the Place Royale
(Place de Vosges) and Place Vendôme in Paris, Cavendish Square in
London, and the Royal Cresent in Bath, a space or sequence of spaces
was planned, the height and scale of the buildings were predeter-
mined, and, in some cases, as with the crescent at Bath and several
squares in London, even the façade (or street wall) of individual
buildings was prescribed. Behind these walls, the buildings were designed in accordance with individual needs, but the elevation of the
façade of each building was subordinated to facilitate the creation of a
public place.

In Paris, Haussmann — not without controversy that has lasted to
this day — superimposed a pattern of streets and public spaces. New
structures that were limited in height, building line, and profile were
constructed accordingly. This unity was reinforced by a vocabulary
of building details: the French window, railings, mansard roofs,
and stone walls. No two buildings are exactly the same, and yet with
all these slight variations there is a wonderful ensemble. Street
façades were dictated for certain streets and avenues, however, to em-

Aerofilms

Individual buildings contribute to the design of the public realm. Arcades, public shelter, and enclosures are recurring themes. Each individual building is subordinated to contribute to the urban whole. The sum total is indeed greater than the parts.

Left:
Aibar, Spain.

Below left:
The King's Circus, Bath. The public realm was designed before the individual buildings.

Below:
Telc, Czechoslovakia.

phasize their importance. The Rue de Rivoli with its arcade along the Louvre, the Place Vendôme, and the Place de Vosges are examples of this and are set apart from other places in the city.

The French had the values, restraint, and *joie de vivre* to build these wonderful streets and to use the Seine, the geometry of corners, and street intersections to their full potential. What happened to this sensibility? Why have vulgar high-rise towers been allowed to spring up all over Paris, disrupting the urban fabric? Obscene and pitiful buildings, they are like a cancer; and you cannot put foreign cells in the body and expect the body to keep working. Placing the Montparnasse Tower on the Rive Gauche in Paris makes this kind of impact. Streets that were designed for a certain density of traffic before the advent of cars suddenly had to accommodate themselves to ten thousand people coming out of a single entrance onto the sidewalk, or to thousands of cars and taxis concentrated at one point. We have, of course, done the same thing to almost every older city in the world. In Paris, which is a city enjoyed and admired by all, however, these acts are particularly incomprehensible.

But this disastrous expression of values is not limited to the older parts of the city. For instance, there is the new residential and commercial area called La Défense, which was built on the axis of the Place de la Concord and the Arc de Triomphe. If we could come to understand how such unfortunate planning occurs, we might be able to put our finger on the forces that responsible urban design must contend with.

Richard Sennett observed the Défense project from a sociologist's viewpoint in *The Fall of Public Man:*

At La Défense, the grounds around the mass of office towers which compose the complex contain a few stores, but the real purpose is to serve as a pass-through area from car or bus to office building. There is little evidence that the planners of La Défense thought this space had intrinsic value, that people from the various office blocks might want to remain in it. The ground, in the words of one planner, is "the traffic-flow-support-nexus for the vertical whole."[26]

© Ezra Stoller

Above:
Two views of Paris. The Avenue de l'Opéra at the turn of the century. La Défense, circa 1970. Richard Sennett writes of La Défense: "The real purpose is to serve as a pass-through area from car or bus to office building. There is little evidence that the planners of La Défense thought this space had any intrinsic value . . ." The kind of surrealistic half-life that La Défense represents is particularly disconcerting because it exemplifies new, unencumbered developments built with ample resources.

Left:
The Mall, Albany, New York. Empire State Plaza. A leading competitor with La Défense. To quote Gertrude Stein, "There is no there, there."

The kind of surrealistic half-life that La Défense represents (and I could have picked on Houston or Mexico City or Caracas) is particularly disconcerting, because it is a *new,* unencumbered development built with ample resources. Effective, humane cities were constructed throughout the nineteenth century: Haussmann's Paris, for instance, and a number of North American cities — among them New York, Philadelphia, and Montreal. While they had poverty, slums, and all of the problems that accompanied the industrial revolution, they were nevertheless more livable then than today.

What distinguishes the contemporary city and, for that matter, contemporary architecture, or the Modern movement, from the past? In the final analysis, one is left with four forces of change. The first is the advent of the car. The second is the elevator. The third is newly acquired materials and technology. And the fourth and perhaps most subtle change is our attitude toward individuality and its effect on community.

The nineteenth-century builder had only stone, brick, and occasionally wood to choose from. The result was a limited range of building details that, in themselves, created visual unity. The limitation of available materials severely restricted what individuals could do to disrupt the urban fabric. The great variety of materials that are currently available, however, make it possible for anyone to build anything. And each new material evokes its own forms, details, and patterns.

The elevator made it feasible to build high structures. The five-to-seven-story limit prevalent in most cities could now be extended to tens and hundreds of floors. This was perhaps not a disruptive force in itself, but by making possible the close grouping of many tall buildings, it permitted a great concentration of people and traffic. The density created by this new range of building prototypes was without precedent. Often, these new tall structures were built on street patterns created for the pre-elevator city. Elsewhere, as in Houston, the structures have been grouped as appendages to a traffic network. Since the seven-story buildings generated particular street and building patterns, it is reasonable to assume that the tall buildings will do the same, in patterns that we are yet to discover.

The car is both a blessing and a curse. On the one hand, who can deny that it has given us tremendous freedom and mobility? Who is prepared to live without it? On the other hand, we haven't come up with structures or arrangements that accommodate the car and the problems it creates — the need for great areas for movement and storage, and the conflict with pedestrians. Nor is it clear that these problems can ever be resolved.

Certainly there is a contradiction between the problems the elevator and the car have caused. The elevator allows people to be concentrated in a relatively small area, while the car disperses them. The elevator results in an environment in which the car is least able to operate.

While bunched-up skyscrapers are the by-product of the elevator, the "Strip" is the result of the car. We have one tool for concentration and another for dispersal, both of which we exploit to the limit. The result is schizophrenia. The kind of concentration that we create in our downtown areas demands collective (mass) transit. The car, on the other hand, helps create Broadacre City and the Strip, with Los Angeles as the model.

Each of these technological developments raises a set of social issues. The car-dominated Strip is a phenomenon that discourages face-to-face social contact. In the traditional city, everything about the daily routine brings people into contact with one another. When one walks to the corner grocery or goes to the bank, there is contact with the grocer, the bank teller, and other customers. Simply walking on the street means that one meets people one knows. The traditional city is a vehicle for socializing. The car city, however, is the opposite. It prevents us from socializing. We sit in a car in a drive-in church and have no contact with other worshipers. We go to a drive-in bank and deal with a teller behind an armored window. Now that cars

The car-dominated Strip is a phenomenon that discourages face-to-face contact. In the traditional city, everything about the daily routine brings people into contact with one another. In the strip city, one sits in a car in a drive-in church; one goes to a drive-in cinema; one goes to a drive-in bank.

Left:
In the driver's seat. The ultimate in isolation and alienation.

are air-conditioned, there is no face-to-face contact with other drivers at stoplights; we drive in sealed cars behind tinted glass.

I believe that the contact between people in the city is valuable, and I believe that people come to the city because they seek this contact. The car has removed this opportunity for social interaction and has produced undesirable social patterns.

Robert Venturi, Denise Scott Brown, and Stephen Izenour, in *Learning from Las Vegas,*[27] and Rayner Banham, in *Los Angeles,*[28] glorify the Strip as an expression of the vernacular. But it seems to me that they abdicate the responsibility of professionals who are involved with the environment by failing to examine the value system of the Strip phenomenon and its causes and consequences. It is painful to see that patterns which appear, at least to me, to indicate a pathology in our society are examined on purely visual grounds. The Strip results from our reliance on the car for mobility and for providing for our many needs. We use the car as an extension of ourselves, and the Strip accommodates this.

But we cannot ignore the fact that the Strip condones — indeed, depends on — the most inefficient use of energy, by encouraging the car and its single driver to hop from spot to spot. This is a high price for society to pay, but the highest price of all is the ultimate alienation and detachment that the Strip causes. When traditional patterns and values are wiped out, it is reasonable to expect an urbanist to assess critically what is taking its place. It is reasonable to expect and even demand that the critic make the connections between the patterns of life and the patterns of form. Regrettably, in these writings visual patterns are examined with obsession but the repercussions on our lives are ignored.

If sprawl and dispersal have caused the disruption of social patterns, the disproportionate value placed on individuality has furthered this process. The city will never become a place where *the sum total is greater than the parts,* so long as we have this egomaniacal desire, collectively and individually, to stand out and show off. At the

corporate and institutional levels, there is the desire to erect unique
and identifiable buildings using every trick in the book, and thus the
architect is driven to exploit all means, materials, forms, and shapes,
to set new fads and fashions.

A couple of years ago I drove through a quarter of Teheran, looking at villas constructed by the newly rich. One of the gestures that
wealth allowed, or perhaps demanded, was a building that pro-
claimed the new status of its owner. A few months ago I drove
through a similar suburb in Mexico City and experienced a sense of
déjà vu — there were the same unrelated, muscle-flexing demonstra-
tions. Here was a parade of trivia and vanity. The villas ranged from
Petit Trianons, chateaux, and chalets to amazing concoctions of building forms: circles, flying saucers, cylinders, and pyramids made of
materials as diverse as marble, stone, brick, wood, plastic, metal, and
mirror — you name it, one after the other, street after street. There
are similar areas in every urban environment. They are a macrocosm
of our urban ills and a limited demonstration of an unlimited problem — the desire for uniqueness at any price and by any available
means. One must desire to belong to one's community before there
can be any hope that the city will, some day, evoke a sense of
harmony.

Mexican villas built within a
couple of years of one another,
located in the same suburb of
Mexico City, 1979.

6   Contemporary Diagnosis

"At a time when *image* is one of the most frequently used words in American speech and writing, one does not too often come upon the real thing."
— Joseph Epstein[29]

"Modernism has been trivialized. After all, how often can it continue to shock, if there is nothing shocking left? If experiment is the norm, how original can anything new be?" — Daniel Bell[30]

EVERY AGE HAS DEVOTED enormous resources to a few buildings of great importance — temples or pyramids, palaces or cathedrals — spending lavishly and apparently without regard for economy. Each society nevertheless has had to provide shelter for its population, and there the demand for economy is absolute and compelling. In ninety-nine percent of the environment, getting the most with the least materials and energy has always been the rule, just as it is in nature, and for the same reason. Only with the utmost efficiency and economy can natural organisms secure their survival.

It is fairly simple to assess economy in the use of materials. Bee-hives demonstrate an intricate geometry that derives the maximum storage space from the minimum use of wax. But the idea of economy is more complex in the human environment, because of the difficulty of defining needs. Who defines the needs? What is minimum? What are basic requirements and what is luxury?

Today we are dealing with an unprecedented number of people. Consequently, we must also deal with what made these numbers and this civilization possible: modern technology. We could not have achieved our present world population without industrialized agriculture, modern medicine, and modern production techniques, and it is reasonable to say that the provision of shelter for this enormous population will not be achieved without the effective use of technology. As far as the rich, industrialized world is concerned, however, the sense of economy as a force in design has been lost. The wealth concentrated in these few countries has permitted a reckless attitude toward resources that is nowhere more obvious than in the area of energy. In the industrial world, eighty to ninety percent of the world's energy production is consumed to achieve "reasonable" standards of comfort. We spend lavishly, building our glass towers, our suburbs, our endless expressways, and our two-ton cars that move one person about.

The political process of equalizing the distribution of wealth, resources, and energy throughout the world is inevitable. The power struggle between industrialized countries and developing countries, the political relationships that have developed since the Second World War, and the new realization that there is a limit to certain kinds of resources all mean that we will have to deal again with economy as a force in design.

The impact of economy extends to the world of style and image. We are all familiar with the Beaux Arts notion of axial, symmetrical design. We rarely see axial, symmetrical designs in indigenous architecture, however, and for a good reason: Indigenous builders are highly sensitive to the elements, to the movements of the sun, to orientation. The sun's movement in the heavens is not symmetrical, and the architecture that evolves in response to that movement is consequently asymmetrical. The recent tradition of Western design is thus truly formalistic. By designing buildings whose wings face east and west, or north and south, the Beaux Arts architects in essence are saying, "I am designing in a world in which the elements are secondary." This is an arrogant posture of a culture that feels it can ignore nature.

Many people feel there is no need to be more rational about the use of resources and energy. I disagree. Not because I don't like symmetrical buildings or prefer shortage to surplus, or because of any lack of concern, but because I feel that every act of waste has a social price that must be paid in the relation of man to man and man to his world. The emerging feeling that we've gone too far and might damage the planet irreversibly is a healthy reawakening to the understanding that design of the manmade environment must be in harmony with nature's design.

Who defines what the requirements are for building a community?

Let's say that I am designing a community. I present my plans. I want to create a garden for everybody. I want to accommodate the cars. I want to give a little sense of privacy. Sooner or later someone will say that it is too expensive. "Put the cars on the surface! Increase the density! Remove the gardens!" This is an inevitable situation wherever you are creating a basic environment.

Who makes the decisions? Usually it is the developers and the bureaucrats. This holds equally true for capitalist, socialist, and communist countries. In North America the developer buys land and tries to maximize its use. His objective is very simple: to get maximum return on investment. In Israel, by contrast, almost all the land is owned by the National Land Authority and is administered by clerks and functionaries. By virtue of long experience in working with these officials, however, I can testify that they are as aggressive and manipulative about getting the maximum use out of the state's land as if they owned it themselves and pocketed every cent of profit.

The developer's function, then, is to maximize income. In doing so, he is constrained by social, community, and individual goals as they are defined by law. Generally, these involve zoning and health standards and fire and safety regulations — quantitative rather than qualitative requirements. In maximizing return on investment, though, the environmental results are often negative. We should not blame the developer for this: His terms of reference are clear. We should blame ourselves for not having defined the goals. My involvement in large-scale projects almost invariably causes me to deal with a bureaucracy: the Ministry of Housing in Israel, the Ministry of Urbanism in Senegal, the Queen's Bureau in Teheran, the Ministry of State for Urban Affairs in Canada. In each case, it is the bureaucracy that attempts to define requirements. And time and time again, it becomes evident that when the user is removed from the process of defining needs, and this process is placed in the hands of a functionary, a situation is created in which the real needs of the user are compromised. And this is because the functionary usually has only two goals in mind — the path of least resistance and the perpetuation of the system.

I am presently designing a school in Baltimore. The school board wants an open-classroom system that will accommodate 150 children per class. The reason for this is that the teacher motivation is poor, and as a result four or five teachers will work together with each of these enormous groups. Since the board can't rely on the quality of teachers, it claims that open classrooms enable the system to accept and work with teachers of lower quality. Where is the child left in all of this? What about his education? At face value, it appears that the child's welfare is in mind. It seems that given the present conditions, the open classroom will result in the best education. But further examination shows that administrative convenience prevails. If smaller groupings are more conducive to a young child's learning process, then the onus is on the administration to invest the energy to train teachers accordingly. That would, of course, demand greater resources in the training of teachers, which, in turn, brings us in a vicious circle to a decision made for administrative convenience — a decision neither the child nor the parent nor, for that matter, the teacher would advocate, if asked.

Here is another example: When designing houses for Inuit families in northern Canada, I attempted to define lifestyle and family needs, and their relation to the village context. Functionaries of the Northwest Territories government chose to abandon the project, because, they claimed, there were not enough resources to meet these needs. At issue was not only the cost of the units but the fact that they departed rather radically from the conventional three-bedroom house normally found in Canadian suburbs. Once again, the citizen whose life was being affected was removed from the decision-making process. In the first place, the administration decided to disrupt the nomadic lifestyle of the Inuit. Having deprived them of their traditional lifestyle, houses nicknamed "matchboxes" were constructed. These ignored the fact that separate bedrooms and the division of the house into several tiny rooms are irrelevant to the Inuit family. Simultaneously, an elaborate welfare network of education, health care, and other services was established, again following conventional patterns imported from the south. The houses I had designed met with strong community approval. The government's decision that they were excessively costly was the result of a value judgment as to how resources should be spent on this community. As it turned out, houses of conventional design were eventually built at similar cost.

The result of all this is that the force of economy in design is totally negative in our culture. Rather than defining objectives and then applying ingenuity, inventiveness, and technology as a means of achieving them, we take the easy way out by compromising on the goals. Why break one's back to find better materials or more efficient ways to enclose or heat space, when the bureaucracy will simply ignore the basic requirements?

It is essential to reverse this procedure and allow the users to participate in the decision-making process. Only then will we create a situation in which the force of economy is a positive one that will restore the healthy conflict between needs and means. Such an interaction will challenge the architect and builder and developer to extend the building process so as to achieve the most with the least, rather than achieve economies at the expense of quality.

In the last ten years, we have seen communities begin to participate in decisions about the environment. This process has been accompanied by a great deal of phony public relations, pseudoparticipation, and, in some cases, manipulation of the communities. But nevertheless, whereas fifteen years ago a bureaucratic authority could run an expressway through a city and destroy several neighborhoods, it cannot do so today. And now developers complain that it's impossible to build in certain cities. "Regulations are complicated, it's hard to get permits," they say. "That's why we are moving to Houston; we can't build in Toronto [or Boston, or Philadelphia] anymore." What they are really saying is that social goals are being defined in these places, and that it is more comfortable to work in places where social and community goals have not been defined at all.

In the last decade, new attitudes have emerged among architects, particularly in the United States. Although these attitudes are quite diverse, critics have grouped them into an overall category under the banner of Postmodernism. Much has been written lately in an attempt to define Postmodernist attitudes. Critics place Philip Johnson in this group, with his AT&T building in New York and his Pittsburgh Glass building in Pittsburgh, as well as Robert Venturi and

Pittsburgh Glass Company Headquarters, Pittsburgh, Pennsylvania. Philip Johnson, architect.

Denise Scott Brown, with their vernacular and mannered architecture and their admiration for Las Vegas and the Strip. Some of these architects are manipulating the forms of the architecture of the 1920s and 1930s. Others are fascinated by neoclassicism and other forms of historicism. Several are involved in literal metaphors: whimsy architecture, joke architecture. They make buildings look as if they have been through an earthquake or are half-collapsed, so that people remember them and come to shop there. Still others have pursued a personal style, expressed primarily in graphic language — a painter's approach to building. And others are pursuing a more recent kind of historicism that verges on neofascism.

I am very disturbed by these attitudes — even more disturbed than by the shortcomings of the Modern movement that preceded them. At the risk of generalizing, I would say that they represent an escapist world of personal indulgence, and are the reaction of those who feel frustrated by their inability to deal with large issues. If one cannot deal effectively with the problems of housing a community, it is obviously easier to deal with housing a client on a ten-acre lot by the sea or, better yet, housing a nonexistent client on a nonexistent site near a nonexistent beach, in a house that will never be built because it will remain on paper. One can put all one's energy into executing a drawing of a house so elegantly that the drawing can be sold to a gallery for a price greater than the fee one would earn for building the house. Architectural drawings are "in." In itself, this is a harmless matter — except when the drawing, which is a tool for building, becomes an end in itself.

One might argue in defense of Postmodern architects that the type of projects they engage in reflect the commissions available to them, rather than their personal preferences. There is evidence, however, to indicate otherwise. In the past, architects faced with building recessions often used their time to develop projects that seemed to be of greatest priority. Even when building activity ceased, as in the Second World War, the avant garde was busy developing proposals that

Building for Best Products Company. A competition exhibited in the Museum of Modern Art, March 1980. It is to be expected that the merchandising house would seek the best talent to concoct images and forms to promote the sale of its products. But it is somewhat surprising that these architects respond enthusiastically to the challenge. It is very surprising that the Museum of Modern Art finds these exercises worthy of the attention of a special exhibit. It is a mark of the times that the architects involved find a merchandising and advertising exercise a suitable vehicle for their preoccupations and interests.

Above left:
SITE Architects, *Indeterminate Façade Showroom,* Houston, Texas.

Above right:
Stanley Tigerman, *The Best Home of All.*

Below left:
Robert A. M. Stern, *The Earth, the Temple, and the Goods.*

Below right:
Allan Greenberg. Proposal for Best Products Company showroom.

demonstrated a social commitment and a concern for the community at large. Each line, each drawing, and every word written amplified this commitment. In fact, architects have been surprisingly inventive at obtaining commissions for what they really care about. During recent recessions, however, as architects developed projects on their own rather than as a response to specific commissions, they typically chose projects devoid of any social, political, economic, or, for that matter, technological or geographical concern. Commissions that architects decades ago would have given low priority, or perhaps even rejected — for example, using architecture as a vehicle for advertising promotion (the Best Products Company stores) or corporate notoriety (the AT&T building) — today elicit the response of the new "avant garde."

The Postmodernists not only tend to pick problems that allow them to sidestep urgent social and economic issues — problems of population density, community and privacy, energy, minimum environmental standards, urbanization patterns, and, notwithstanding their claims, regional contexts — but also have demonstrated an aversion to the traditional ingredients of style. Their visual outputs — be it the re-creation of ancient Egyptology in soft pastel color façades; the intricate three-dimensional sculptural reworking of the early International style; the more directly eclectic reproduction of historical details, ranging from Art Deco to neoclassicism to Palladio; or the use of a building as an opportunity for literal commentary or metaphor — have not been generated by materials, construction, structural systems, the placement of the building on site, or the urban context.

The Modern movement has had its shortcomings. Examples are Le Corbusier's utopian schemes for the Ville Radieuse, whose towers rise out of a park; the wholesale rejection of traditional urban fabric; the refusal to recognize people's needs for decoration and ornament; the diagrammatic response to complex desires and aspirations; and even the formalism of an "international" style that created its own tyranny. But the Modern movement was born out of a sense of social responsibility, out of a feeling that environmental solutions had to provide for the whole population, and that architects must be involved with society as a whole, not just with erecting monuments and mansions for a very small segment of the population. The movement grew out of a conviction that technology could be harnessed to respond to these needs. Yet we recognize many ways in which they failed: Many buildings of the time were pseudotechnological (hand-built out of block and plaster to look like machine-made products); and the need for correct orientation and exposure to the sun, although stated in every manifesto, was demonstrated in practice by lining buildings up in rows like soldiers facing north-south, as if the sun were stationary in the south.

James Marston Fitch recently wrote in the *AIA Journal:*

A truly objective re-examination of the past 50 years of modern architecture would reveal that its failures are due not to its having been "too functional" but to its having been not functional enough . . . the interconnection of form and function was indissoluble.[31]

The fact is that the Postmodernists choose to say "Down with the Modern movement," rather than to say "They had many shortcomings; where can we improve upon them?" Once again, instead of treating design as evolution (as indigenous builders always did), the Postmodernists are concerned only with new inventions on a tabula rasa.

My criticism would tend to be more gentle if it were felt that Postmodernist concerns are primarily reactions, based on human considerations, to the errors of the Modern movement. But in fact, as many practitioners would confess, much of their recent work is rooted in the cult of personality — in the narcissistic desire to make something new for the sake of something new, for the sake of being recognized (even if notoriously so). And to achieve this, the professional press is manipulated — in fact, it begs to be manipulated, committed as it is to finding new styles, fads, and fashions — fre-

Luckhardt Brothers. Residential district with tower houses, 1927. The Modern movement had its shortcomings. The diagrammatic solution to complex needs, and even the formalism of style, created their own tyranny. "Re-examination of the past 50 years of modern architecture would reveal that its failures are due not to its having been 'too functional' but to its having been not functional enough." James Marston Fitch.

quently enough to keep circulation high and advertisers happy.

This recalls the basic issue discussed earlier: the place of the designer. To quote Ackerman again:

The autonomy and authority given to the designer by the tradition of European aesthetics might be restrained in the interests of the community. This involves both the pragmatic formulation of the design process as a transactional field and the moral formulation of a complementarity between the designer's power of free imagination and his responsibility toward the whole company of those affected by his invention.[32]

I have a great deal of trust in the judgment of the man in the street. We must be more attentive to his views. The public rebels against the glass box, is unhappy with the formalistic solutions of contemporary architecture, and talks about modern architecture being cold. It reacts against urban solutions that it considers to be inhuman, as it does against high-rise public-housing projects. I personally believe that these reactions are valid.

The Postmodernists share these concerns in part, but the tragedy is that their reaction has been to turn inward. Frank Gehry put forward his views in a recent lecture at Harvard:

I try to rid myself . . . of the burden of culture . . . I want to be openended. There are no rules, no right or wrong.

James M. Fitch summed up the opposing position:

After half a century during which the profession was committed to helping society in a rational solution to its architectural needs, we are now being urged to abandon — indeed to reverse — that course.

The Postmodernists are now telling us that content and expression, function and form, have no more fundamental a connection in architecture than in scene painting, dressmaking or hat design.[33]

The Postmodernists' preoccupation with abstract visual patterns, graphic gamesmanship, and eclectic exercises diverts their attention so that they do not tackle the tough issues, confront the bureaucracy,

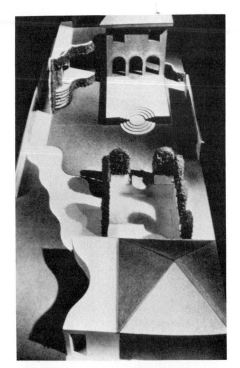

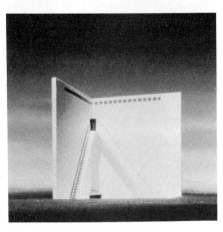

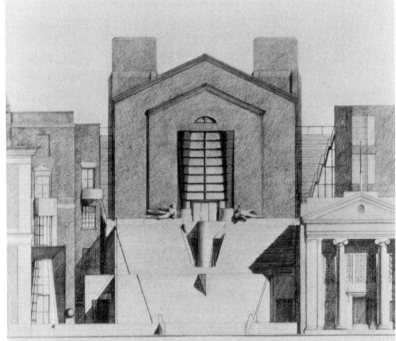

MEMORIAL HALL FACADE

Progressive Architecture Annual Awards, 1980. A blend of literal metaphors, whimsy, appliqués, and eclecticism. "The Postmodernists are now telling us that content and expression, function and form, have no more fundamental a connection in architecture than in scene painting, dressmaking or hat design." James Marston Fitch.

Far left (above): Stanley Tigerman & Associates, *A Kosher Kitchen for a Suburban Jewish American Princess,* Wilmette, Ill. Architectural Design Award.

Above left: Michael Graves, *House in Green Brook, N.J.* Architectural Design Award.

Far left (below): Emilio Ambasz, *House for a Couple,* Córdoba, Spain. Architectural Design Award.

Below left: Machado and Silvetti, *The Steps of Providence,* Providence, R.I. First Award.

Right: Venturi, Rauch and Scott Brown, *House in New Castle City,* Delaware. Architectural Design Award.

or risk losing clients. One can, of course, consider this cause and effect in reverse. Frustrated by their inability to deal effectively with social and economic issues, the forces of ecology and energy, the problems of demography and density, deeply pessimistic of the opportunity for satisfaction in this context, they turn in relief to abstract visual patterns, graphic gamesmanship, and eclectic exercises. It is easier to deal with the particular, the personal, and the isolated than to deal with the collective and with what is part of the greater context. It is easier to build a house in the countryside than to build one that must relate to other houses in a community. It is easier to deal with the needs of an individual (particularly if he is wealthy) than with the needs of a community (particularly if it is poor).

This attitude has had a disturbing impact on students. Students are always eager to learn of new trends, but they are also eternally frustrated about the gap between utopian dreams and reality, between what they would like to achieve and what they can in fact accomplish.

In the sixties, students of architecture were immersed in the social concerns of the time but avoided the difficult task of synthesizing these concerns into three-dimensional proposals — the ultimate test as to whether the bridge between program and buildable form can be made. By sticking to bubble diagrams and verbal statements, they expressed their intentions but failed to synthesize them. The seventies were marked by a renewed interest in drawing and the craft of building. This occurred just as new and tough environmental issues emerged. The broad impact of the energy crisis, the general recession in the economy, diminished funds available for building, and the sense of failure of the Great Society of the Lyndon Johnson era all led to increased pessimism. In this context, students grasped Postmodernist doctrine as a drowning man grasps a life preserver. It is no coincidence that the nonconfrontation doctrines of Postmodernism emerged in the midst of the economic upheaval of the seventies.

There are many reasons why the Postmodernist doctrine can be one of nonconfrontation. It deals with problems that are not socially charged. The problems of designing a community, the confrontation between economics and amenities, between building form and energy consumption, are avoided. Projects are chosen in which the program is sufficiently neutral so as to contain a small number of constraints. Then too, there is the use or misuse of history. The history of architecture and urbanism, the understanding of the evolution of building form and the ability to derive lessons for building today, have always been essential ingredients of the architect's education. Even in the early decades of the century, when history was played down, architects never failed to draw upon this reservoir. Today, however, the student treats history as a bag of tricks. Rather than understand the evolution of building and urbanism, the relationship between context and form, the causal aspects of the evolution of building, he is allowed, indeed encouraged, to dive in and pick up, willy-nilly, a motif out of history to be reproduced and elaborated upon. Thus we find parts or wholes of buildings, or sometimes even details such as moldings, reproduced and transformed in scale, not only out of context but without the understanding of what brought them about in the first place.

There is a similar attitude toward symbolism. Having stated that the Modern movement was deprived of symbolic gestures, Postmodernist doctrine confuses genuine universal symbols, ones that are immediately meaningful to people from a particular culture, with ironic metaphors — symbols that are "in" and familiar to a particular group while totally meaningless to the public at large. An example is a golden TV antenna placed over the roof of a home for the elderly — a gesture that might be meaningful to a limited circle of architects, but certainly one that lacks universality. For the students, however, there is solace in this introversion, since it is easier to draw upon one's immediate circle than to study and penetrate one's society in order to gain an understanding of meaningful symbols.

Finally, there is the surface treatment that is characteristic of Postmodernism. In the recent past, architects had the ambition to evolve building forms that would be instruments of social change. Architects permitted themselves to be the interpreters of a program, and to mold buildings in response to their own interpretations, often with far-reaching economic and operational consequences. More recently, governments, corporate clients, and developers have increasingly lessened the architect's involvement with program definition, increasingly clipping his wings. Architects are told by developers that an office building shall be no more or less than 25,000 square feet per floor. They are given precise definition of the plan and form of a hotel, government complex, or residential building. As one colleague said to me recently, "What is left but the design of the skin?" Given social and cultural needs, this situation is intolerable, but Postmodernist doctrine diffuses this frustration by emphasizing the role an architect must play in designing the skin. The students, affected equally by the new rules, now relax about the packaged building formulas that everyone around them seems to be saddled with, and enjoy the makeup job. It does not really matter that the contribution under such circumstances can only be skin deep. New criteria of subtlety are created so that, for example, making a glass curtain wall with colored glass panels rather than metal ones, or with colored mullions rather than ones made from aluminum, or with a special new type of mirror glass, or with multichromatic moldings, becomes a significant development worthy of great appreciation.

I have stated that urgent issues are being neglected. Let me attempt to define them. One of the toughest issues of our time is that of scale and numbers. The millions of people living together in cities and using transit systems, the tens of thousands of students in universities, and the untold numbers of patients in hospitals present new problems. The population is larger than ever before and is living in closer proximity. The difficulty of attaining certain amenities is therefore greater. Coming to terms with the age of big numbers is a design problem at the most profound level, posing issues about patterns of settlement, size and scale of cities, and concentration or dispersal on a global scale that has no precedent.

Directly related to this is the pressure toward greater population density. We had the illusion some years back that we could all live on our two-acre plots, but we are increasingly coming to realize that we do not have that choice now, that there is neither the means (energy) nor the will to continue to disperse. In the growing centers of population, including those in developing countries, the things people want out of life, work, and education are attainable only in the large cities, where people are closely packed together.

To achieve privacy within densely populated areas and to create a sense of territoriality for the family and the individual are very difficult design problems. Bureaucracies limit the range of answers by imposing constraints, but the proliferation of bureaucracies has not reduced our desire for a sense of uniqueness, our demand for greater choice, or our need to consume and live in ways that we perceive to be special to ourselves.

Another issue is that of living in a synthetic environment as opposed to living in closer harmony with nature. Is it important to have a window in a classroom? Is it reasonable to sit all day in a conference room without being able to look out a window? How do we react to an environment in which all the materials are synthetic and lack the textures and warmth of those that are familiar — stone, brick, wood, and wool? There are continuing pressures inherent in the fact that we are running out of natural materials and must increasingly depend on synthetics. In designing new types of buildings, it seems easiest to give up any attempt to connect to the outdoors. The typical office-building floor, which once was 8000 to 12,000 square feet in area, is now as large as 25,000 square feet; in five years this area will comprise 50,000 or 100,000 square feet, as more and more indoor offices are imposed for bureaucratic and administrative expediency.

Certain traditional ways of making things have died out, and we are entering a period in which modern production systems, mass production, and automation will play an important part in manufacturing the environment. These techniques have their own tyranny. For example, although the stamping machine is a good, fast way to

4 Each dwelling should have direct access to a private, furnishable outdoor garden, court, terrace, atrium, balcony, or roof space, preferably open to the sky.

In housing of one or two storys there should be gardens or courtyards. In medium and high-rise housing the design of the building should provide for balconies, terraces or usable roof areas.

Furnishable means that the family has enough space to sit around a table in comfort.

In addition to the usable outdoor space,

conveniently located vegetable garden plots should be made available to the residents of medium and high-rise buildings not in contact with the ground.

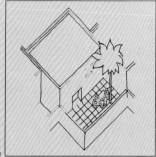

50 The family garden - a
51 usable outdoor space.
52

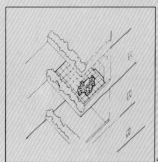

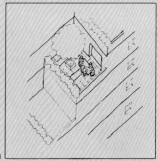

53 Roof terraces offer a
54 solution to the family
55 outdoor living space in
   the highrise structure.

50

51

52

53

54

55

Sample page from "The Habitat Bill of Rights." In all, "The Habitat Bill of Rights" comprised 180 pages, with 47 specific recommendations dealing with scale of room, dwelling, cluster, pedestrian precinct, and community. "The Habitat Bill of Rights" was written by a committee appointed by the International Congress of Architects at Persepolis in September 1974, the working members being: Nader Ardalan, Georges Candilis, Balkrishna Doshi, Moshe Safdie, and Josep Lluis Sert.

shape metal, it also imposes the tyranny of standardization: Each piece of shaped metal is identical. The extrusion machine produces identical moldings. It takes inventiveness and conscious effort to control these mass-production systems so that they will give us the kind of variety and choice we want. "In civilized society the rule is the limitless production of the same product," Octavio Paz has written. "Mass production is based on the idea of maximum consumption and the product's minimum durability. In Harmony (a utopian vision of Fourier's) we find the rule inverted; an immense variety of products of great durability and minimum consumption."[34]

These are very complicated design issues, each of which should give us a lifetime of challenge — and they have little to do with Palladio or the Strip or, for that matter, Albert Speer. The new technology of building will generate its own rich, visual language of building forms and methods. Instead of emphasizing our self-expression as designers, the new technology will be a vehicle for methods that will come to terms with today's problems and lead to a more collective mode of expression.

It is for this reason that indulgence is dangerous and needs to be exposed. The risk that gifted people will divert themselves from where their attention and energy should go is too high a price to pay.

Man's development has been a journey toward greater individuality and freedom. If we compare ourselves to the free citizens of Rome or ancient Egypt, not to mention their slaves, we realize that we have a freedom that transcends our sense of obligation to the community. In our striving for greater individuality and freedom, however, we have become caught in a vicious circle. In terms of mobility, we have developed the car only to find ourselves in traffic jams. We strive for freedom from hunger, and then have obesity to worry about. We strive for freedom of information, and suffer from information overload. We strive for a society in which there is social mobility and then find ourselves friendless. We strive for sexual freedom and find ourselves deprived of the institution of the family and bored by pornography.

It is in this context that we must reconsider, and search for the proper balance between self and community. What is wrong is that we have put a great deal of energy into defining individual goals and securing the right of individuals to set their own goals, but have neglected to define community goals. As Christopher Lasch points out in *The Culture of Narcissism,* the obsession with self has become the dominant force in our times.[35]

The real difference between indigenous towns and our own strips and suburbs is that indigenous towns were communities; what their inhabitants built expressed a sense of community, while what we build today does not. We do not feel that we are part of the community, and what we do with our physical environment expresses this.

In *Beyond Habitat,* I talked about an Environmental Bill of Rights.[36] I called it the Habitat Code. Later on, after I attended a conference in Iran and shared this thought with a number of friends — Josep Lluis Sert, Nader Ardalan, and B. V. Doshi — we decided to try to reach a consensus about the goals to be achieved when building a community. We came from different cultures: Ardalan, who was educated in the West, is Middle Eastern in background; Doshi is from a poor and developing India; Sert a Spaniard who has decades of practice in America; and I have an East-West background. Could consensus be achieved? We spent two years in frequent meetings, discussing and writing a document in which we attempted to deal with qualitative questions. It was an attempt at defining shared objectives for improving the building environment. We thought that once we had written it, we could disseminate it widely and ask people to respond and tell us where they shared our views and where they disagreed. Here was an opportunity to begin to counter the bureaucracy. At the very least, the document could initiate healthy dialogue about our goals and desires, on one hand, and the limitations of our resources, on the other.

We thought that there would be an immediate demand for a hundred thousand copies to be printed and distributed. But the Code was treated with cool interest at the U.N. Habitat conference in Vancouver in 1976, and we never found a publisher who could see in it more than limited professional interest. We continue in our endeavor. Each of us still believes that only by defining these goals in clear, everyday language will we ever arrive at collective agreements.

City master plans, as they have traditionally been drawn, are wishy-washy land-use documents that determine little about the goals of the community and its environment. They consistently use the same colors: yellow for housing, red for commercial use, blue for institutions, purple for industry, and green for parks. They do not define whether the yellow represents high-rise cliffs or small patio houses, nor do they indicate whether these places are good to be in or bad to be in. They do not specify whether the red constitutes a bazaar, a small neighborhood center, or an enormous shopping center surrounded by parking space for five thousand cars. Even where it is colored green, the plan does not clarify whether the place is one where people can enjoy the outdoors, or whether it represents vacant land that is unfit for human use, as are the many so-called parks and open spaces between our expressways.

In Jerusalem, I came to realize that master plans are not merely flawed; as tools for the expression of community needs, they are impotent and exert little influence on the quality of life. They are far from being a means by which the community can express its aspirations. And it seems to me that if there is one place we should now focus our attention, it is on creating the circumstances by which we can define collective goals and invent a new kind of master plan, a new kind of process that will guide us in the building of the environment. Individual desires must no longer be the guide.

As Richard Sennett aptly put it:

To make modern cities serve human needs, we shall have to change the way in which city planners work. Instead of planning for some abstract urban whole, planners are going to have to work for the concrete parts of the city, the different classes, ethnic groups, and races it contains. And the work they do for these people cannot be laying out their future; the people will have no chance to mature unless they do that for themselves, unless they are actively involved in shaping their social lives.[37]

When a mosque was built in a village, the people built it together. If they decided to create a market square, there must have been a mechanism for arriving at a consensus, whether it was a village meeting or some other medium. We need to define shared goals and then find a way to have these goals translated into working documents for the city. Then, perhaps, we can resolve the question of how five architects — or a hundred architects or, for that matter, a hundred designers, some of whom might not be architects — can work together to make a neighborhood.

A couple of years ago, my friend Nader Ardalan and I carried on a correspondence that dealt with issues of mutual concern. At one point we discussed the book about Louis Kahn written by August Komendant. Komendant was Kahn's structural engineer and also the engineer for Habitat. He had written a book about his eighteen years with Kahn, in which he made some critical statements about Kahn's attitudes toward design. These upset Ardalan. He wrote me a letter concerning the whole question of personal expression in design. He felt in harmony with the way Kahn spoke of the centrality of expression in design as a generative force of creativity.

Writing to Ardalan one evening from Jerusalem, I attempted to sum up my thoughts and feelings:

He who seeks truth shall find beauty.
He who seeks beauty shall find vanity.
He who seeks order shall find gratification.
He who seeks gratification shall be disappointed.
He who considers himself the servant of his fellow beings shall find the
    joy of self-expression.
He who seeks self-expression shall fall into the pit of arrogance.
Arrogance is incompatible with nature.
Through nature, the nature of the universe and the nature of man, we
    shall seek truth.
If we seek truth, we shall find beauty.

Notes

1. Daniel Bell, *The Cultural Contradictions of Capitalism* (New York: Basic Books, 1978), p. 78.

2. Mary Catherine Bateson, *Our Own Metaphor* (New York: Alfred A. Knopf, 1972), p. 236.

3. D'Arcy Thompson, *On Growth and Form* (New York: Cambridge University Press, 1959).

4. Andreas Feininger, *The Anatomy of Nature* (London: Thomas Yoseloff, Ltd., 1956).

5. Carl Sagan, *The Dragons of Eden* (New York: Random House, 1977).

6. Octavio Paz, "Eroticism and Gastrosophy," *Daedalus* (Fall 1972): 72.

7. Bernard Rudofsky, *Architecture Without Architects* (New York: Doubleday & Co., 1969).

8. Nader Ardalan and Laleh Bakhtiar, *The Sense of Unity: The Sufi Tradition in Persian Architecture* (Chicago: University of Chicago Press, 1979).

9. James Marston Fitch, "A Funny Thing Happened . . . ," *AIA Journal* (December 1979).

10. Christopher Alexander and Serge Chermayeff, *Community and Privacy* (New York: Doubleday & Co., 1963).

11. James S. Ackerman, "Transactions in Architectural Design," *Critical Inquiry* (December 1974): 243.

12. Robert Venturi, *Complexity and Contradiction in Architecture* (New York: Museum of Modern Art, 1977).

13. Martin L. Gross, "Germaine Greer, Conversations with an Author," *Book Digest* (January 1980): 32.

14. Ibid.

15. Ayn Rand, *The Fountainhead* (New York: New American Library, 1943).

16. Gross, "Germaine Greer," p. 34.

17. Rollo May, *The Courage to Create* (New York: Norton, 1975), p. 149.

18. Gunther Stent, *The Coming of the Golden Age* (New York: Natural History Press, 1969), p. 98.

19. Ibid., p. 104.

20. James S. Ackerman, "On Judging Art Without Absolutes," *Critical Inquiry* (Spring 1979).

21. Christopher Lasch, *The Culture of Narcissism* (New York: Warner Books, 1979), p. 86.

22. Paz, "Eroticism and Gastrosophy," p. 68.

23. Bernard Rudofsky, *Are Clothes Modern?* (Chicago: P. Theobold, 1947).

24. *Toronto Globe and Mail,* February 23, 1980.

25. From *Q & A,* a film about Charles Eames. Distributed by Herman Miller, New York.

26. Richard Sennett, *The Fall of Public Man* (New York: Vintage Books, 1974), p. 14.

27. Robert Venturi, Denise Scott Brown, and Stephen Izenour, *Learning from Las Vegas* (Cambridge, Mass.: MIT Press, 1972).

28. Reyner Banham, *Los Angeles* (New York: Harper and Row, 1971).

29. Lasch, *The Culture of Narcissism,* p. 184.

30. Bell, *The Cultural Contradictions of Capitalism,* p. xxvi.

31. Fitch, "A Funny Thing Happened . . . ," p. 83.

32. Ackerman, "Transactions in Architectural Design," p. 241.

33. Fitch, "A Funny Thing Happened . . . ," p. 84.

34. Paz, "Eroticism and Gastrosophy," p. 73.

35. Lasch, *The Culture of Narcissism,* p. 87.

36. Moshe Safdie, *Beyond Habitat* (Cambridge, Mass.: MIT Press, 1970).

37. Sennett, *The Fall of Public Man,* p. 102.

Selected Bibliography

James S. Ackerman, *The Architecture of Michelangelo* (New York: Viking Press, 1961).
———. *Palladio* (New York: Penguin Books, 1967).
Christopher Alexander, *The Oregon Experiment* (New York: Oxford University Press, 1975).
———. *A Pattern Language* (New York: Oxford University Press, 1977).
———. *A Timeless Way of Building* (New York: Oxford University Press, 1979).
Christopher Alexander and Serge Chermayeff, *Community and Privacy* (New York: Doubleday & Co., 1963).
Nader Ardalan and Laleh Bakhtiar, *The Sense of Unity: The Sufi Tradition in Persian Architecture* (Chicago: University of Chicago Press, 1979).
Reyner Banham, *Los Angeles* (New York: Harper and Row, 1971).
Gregory Bateson, *Mind and Nature* (New York: E. P. Dutton, 1979).
Mary Catherine Bateson, *Our Own Metaphor* (New York: Alfred A. Knopf, 1972).
Daniel Bell, *The Cultural Contradictions of Capitalism* (New York: Basic Books, 1978).
Italo Calvino, *Invisible Cities* (New York: Harcourt Brace Jovanovich, 1972).
Norma Evenson, *Paris: A Century of Change, 1878–1978* (New Haven, Conn.: Yale University Press, 1979).
Andreas Feininger, *The Anatomy of Nature* (London: Thomas Yoseloff, Ltd., 1956).
E. H. Gombrich, *The Sense of Order* (Ithaca, N.Y.: Cornell University Press, 1979).

Germaine Greer, *The Obstacle Race* (New York: Farrar, Straus & Giroux, 1979).

Anne Hollander, *Seeing Through Clothes* (New York: Viking Press, 1978).

Rachel H. Kemper, *Costume* (New York: Newsweek Books, 1979).

Ralph Knowles, *Energy and Form* (Cambridge, Mass.: MIT Press, 1974).

August E. Komendant, *Eighteen Years with Architect Louis I. Kahn* (Englewood, N.J.: Aloray Publishing Co., 1975).

Susan K. Langer, *Philosophy in a New Key* (Cambridge, Mass.: Harvard University Press, 1942).

Christopher Lasch, *The Culture of Narcissism* (New York: Warner Books, 1979).

Benoit B. Mandelbrot, *Fractals* (San Francisco: W. H. Freeman & Co., 1977).

Rollo May, *The Courage to Create* (New York: Norton, 1975).

Museum of Modern Art, *Building for Best Products* (New York, 1979).

George Nelson, *How to See* (Boston: Little, Brown & Co., 1977).

———. *On Design* (Boston: Watson-Guptill Publications, 1979).

John Pile, *Design: Purpose, Form and Meaning* (Amherst, Mass.: University of Massachusetts Press, 1979).

Ayn Rand, *The Fountainhead* (New York: New American Library, 1943).

Bernard Rudofsky, *Architecture Without Architects* (New York: Doubleday & Co., 1969).

———. *Are Clothes Modern?* (Chicago: P. Theobold, 1947).

———. *The Prodigious Builders* (New York: Harcourt Brace Jovanovich, 1977).

———. *Streets for People* (New York: Doubleday & Co., 1969).

Carl Sagan, *Broca's Brain* (New York: Random House, 1979).

———. *The Dragons of Eden* (New York: Random House, 1977).

Richard Sennett, *The Fall of Public Man* (New York: Vintage Books, 1974).

———. *The Uses of Disorder* (New York: Vintage Books, 1970).

Herbert A. Simon, *The Sciences of the Artificial* (Cambridge, Mass.: MIT Press, 1969).

D. K. Spector, *Urban Spaces* (Greenwich, Conn.: New York Graphic Society, 1974).

Peter Stevens, *Patterns in Nature* (Boston: Little, Brown & Co., 1974).

Gunther Stent, *The Coming of the Golden Age* (New York: Natural History Press, 1969).

Lewis Thomas, *The Medusa and the Snail* (New York: Viking Press, 1974).

D'Arcy Thompson, *On Growth and Form* (New York: Cambridge University Press, 1959).

Robert Venturi, *Complexity and Contradiction in Architecture* (New York: Museum of Modern Art, 1977).

Robert Venturi, Denise Scott Brown, and Stephen Izenour, *Learning from Las Vegas* (Cambridge, Mass.: MIT Press, 1972).

Tom Wolfe, *The Painted Word* (New York: Farrar, Straus & Giroux, 1976).

Francis A. Yates, *The Art of Memory* (Chicago: University of Chicago Press, 1966).

Credits

Unless otherwise indicated, the credit for a particular page applies to all photographs on that page.

page

2   Andreas Feininger, *The Anatomy of Nature* (Crown Publishers, New York, 1956).

4   *Top left.* Andreas Feininger. By permission of Life Picture Service, Time, Inc.

4   *Top right.* Andreas Feininger, *The Anatomy of Nature* (Crown Publishers, New York, 1956).

4   *Bottom.* Peter Stevens

6   © Judy MacCready, 1977

8   *Top.* David Litz

8   *Bottom.* Courtesy of "Julia Child & Co.," by James Scherer for WGBH, Boston.

10   Andreas Feininger, *The Anatomy of Nature* (Crown Publishers, New York, 1956).

12   *Top left.* David Litz

12   *Top right.* Illustration from Gordon Lynn Walls, *Vertebrate Eye and Its Adaptive Radiation* (Cranbrook Institute of Science, Bloomfield Hills, Mich., 1942), as modified from Maximilian Salzmann, 1912.

12   *Bottom left. Sweet's Catalogue*

12   *Bottom right.* David Litz

16   Courtesy of Bell Laboratories, Short Hills, N.J.

18–44   Moshe Safdie

45   *Top.* D. K. Specter, *Urban Spaces* (New York Graphic Society, Greenwich, Conn., 1974).

45   *Bottom.* Moshe Safdie

46   Peter Blake

50   *Top.* Henry A. Millon, *Baroque and Rococo Architecture* (George Braziller, New York, 1967).

50   *Bottom.* Pepi Merisio

52   *Left.* Pepi Merisio

52   *Right.* Gabinetto fotografico della Soprintendenza ai Beni Artistici e Storici di Firenze.

53   *Left.* Alinari/Editorial Photocolor Archives

53   *Right.* Photograph by courtesy of Electa Editrice, Milan, Italy.

56   *Left.* Alinari/Editorial Photocolor Archives

56–57   Leonardo Benevolo, *The Architecture of the Renaissance* (Westview Press, Boulder, Col., 1978).

57   Pepi Merisio

58   Soprintendenza per i Beni Ambientali e Architettonici del Piemonte, Torino, Italy.

59   *Left.* Moshe Safdie

59   *Right.* Photograph by courtesy of Electa Editrice, Milan, Italy.

62   *Top.* Peter Varley

62   *Bottom.* Moshe Safdie

64   John Hancock Mutual Life Insurance Company

65   Gorchev & Gorchev

70   *Wotan,* 1950 (oil on canvas). From the collection of Mr. and Mrs. Robert C. Scull, New York.

71   Murray L. Eiland, *Oriental Rugs* (New York Graphic Society, Boston, 1973).

72   Antonello Perissinotto

73–74   Moshe Safdie

75   *Top.* Arthur Drexler, *The Architecture of Japan* (Museum of Modern Art, New York, 1955).

75   *Bottom.* Rafael Ferrer, *Puerto Rican Sun,* 1979. Reproduced in *Art in America,* March 1980.

page

76 C. D. B. Bryan, *The National Air and Space Museum* (New York, 1979). © Harry N. Abrams, Inc., Publisher.

80 *Top.* Claes Oldenburg, *Falling Fan,* model. Collection of Molly Straeter, New York.

80 *Bottom left.* Andy Warhol, *Soup Can.* Castelli Archives.

80 *Bottom right.* Jasper Johns, *Painted Bronze.* Collection of Mr. and Mrs. Robert C. Scull.

81 Ellsworth Kelly, *Two Panels, Yellow and Black,* 1968. Sidney Janis Gallery, New York.

84 Reprinted by permission of *The Wall Street Journal,* © Dow Jones & Company, Inc., 1980. All rights reserved.

86 *Left.* Ezra Stoller, Esto Photographics, Inc.

86 *Right.* Benjamin Thompson and Associates, Inc.

88 E. Benner

90 *Top left.* United States Steel Corporation

90 *Top right. Progressive Architecture,* January 1979. PPG Industries.

90 *Bottom left.* Balthazar Korab

90 *Bottom right.* Reprinted from *Edward Durrell Stone,* by permission of the publisher, Horizon Press, New York.

92 Moshe Safdie

94 Judy Bing

96 Norman McGrath

102 Moshe Safdie

104 David Litz

106 *Top left.* Moshe Safdie

106 *Bottom left and right.* Reprinted from *The Sense of Unity* by Nader Ardalan and Laleh Bakhtiar, by permission of The University of Chicago Press. © 1973 by The University of Chicago.

108 *Top and bottom right.* Bernard Rudofsky, *Architecture Without Architects* (Doubleday, New York, 1969).

page

108 *Bottom left.* Aerofilms

110 *Top.* Norma Evenson, *Paris: A Century of Change, 1878–1978* (Yale University Press, New Haven, Conn., 1979).

110 *Bottom.* Ezra Stoller, Esto Photographics, Inc.

112 *Top.* George Nelson, *How to See* (Little, Brown & Co., Boston, 1977).

112 *Bottom.* David Litz

114–15 Isaac Franco

122 Reprinted from the July 1979 issue of *Progressive Architecture,* copyright 1979, Reinhold Publishing.

124 *Top left.* SITE Architects. Museum of Modern Art, *Buildings for Best Products.* New York, 1979.

124 *Top right.* Stanley Tigerman. Museum of Modern Art, *Buildings for Best Products,* New York, 1979.

124 *Bottom left.* Robert A. M. Stern. Museum of Modern Art, *Buildings for Best Products.* New York, 1979.

124 *Bottom right.* Allan Greenberg. Museum of Modern Art, *Buildings for Best Products.* New York, 1979.

126 Leonardo Benevolo, *History of Modern Architecture* (MIT Press, Cambridge, Mass., 1971).

128 *Top left.* Stanley Tigerman & Associates, *PA* Annual Awards, 1979.

128 *Top right.* Michael Graves, *PA* Annual Awards, 1979.

128 *Bottom left.* Emilio Ambasz, *PA* Annual Awards, 1979.

128 *Bottom right.* Machado and Silvetti, *PA* Annual Awards, 1979.

129 Venturi, Rauch and Scott Brown, *PA* Annual Awards, 1979.

134 Moshe Safdie *et al., Habitat Bill of Rights,* 1976.